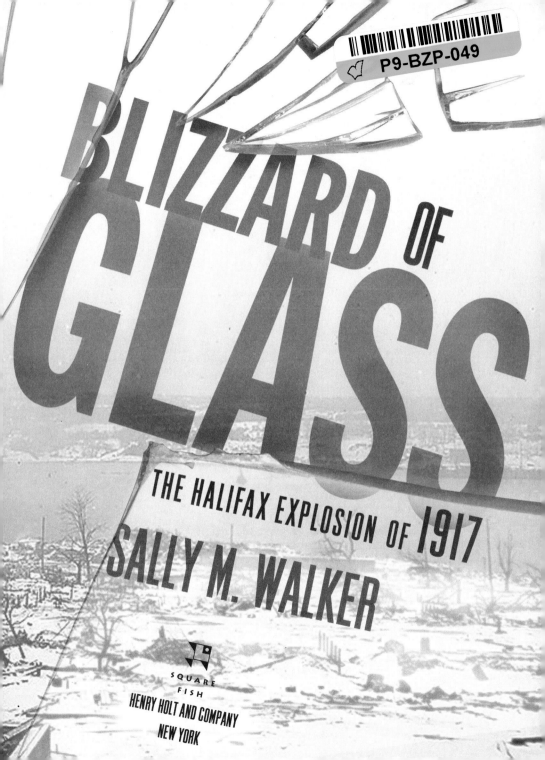

BLIZZARD OF GLASS

THE HALIFAX EXPLOSION OF 1917

SALLY M. WALKER

SQUARE
FISH

HENRY HOLT AND COMPANY
NEW YORK

SQUARE FISH

An Imprint of Macmillan
175 Fifth Avenue
New York, NY 10010
mackids.com

Square Fish and the Square Fish logo are trademarks of Macmillan and
are used by Henry Holt and Company under license from Macmillan.

Square Fish books may be purchased for business or promotional use. For information on bulk
purchases, please contact the Macmillan Corporate and Premium Sales Department at
(800) 221-7945 x 5442 or by e-mail at specialmarkets@macmillan.com.

Library of Congress Cataloging-in-Publication Data
Walker, Sally M.
Blizzard of glass : the Halifax explosion of 1917 / Sally M. Walker.
    p.   cm.
Includes bibliographical references.
ISBN 978-1-250-04008-4 (paperback) / ISBN 978-1-4668-0510-1 (e-book)
1. Halifax Explosion, Halifax, N.S., 1917—Juvenile literature.
2. Halifax (N.S.)—History—20th century—Juvenile literature.
3. Explosions—Nova Scotia—Halifax—History—20th century—Juvenile literature.
4. Halifax (N.S.)—Biography—Juvenile literature.   I. Title.
F1039.5.H17W35 2011   971.6'22503—dc22   2011005914

Originally published in the United States by Henry Holt and Company
First Square Fish Edition: 2014
Book designed by Meredith Pratt
Square Fish logo designed by Filomena Tuosto

1 3 5 7 9 10 8 6 4 2

AR: 7.9 / LEXILE: 1100L

For storytellers, young and old,
who cherish a tale and then share it with others

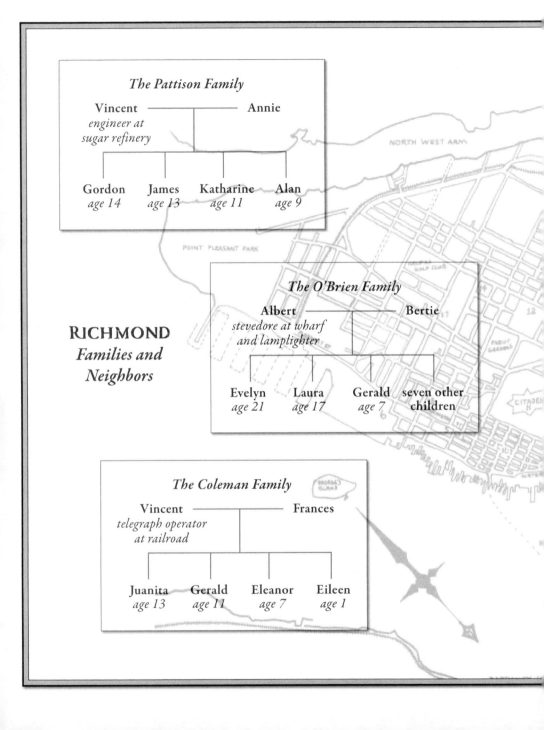

The Pattison Family

Vincent ——————— Annie
engineer at
sugar refinery

Gordon | James | Katharine | Alan
age 14 | *age 13* | *age 11* | *age 9*

The O'Brien Family

Albert ——————— Bertie
stevedore at wharf
and lamplighter

Evelyn | Laura | Gerald | seven other
age 21 | *age 17* | *age 7* | children

RICHMOND
Families and
Neighbors

The Coleman Family

Vincent ——————— Frances
telegraph operator
at railroad

Juanita | Gerald | Eleanor | Eileen
age 13 | *age 11* | *age 7* | *age 1*

NORTH WEST ARM

POINT PLEASANT PARK

FAMILY MEMBERS
Featured in Blizzard of Glass

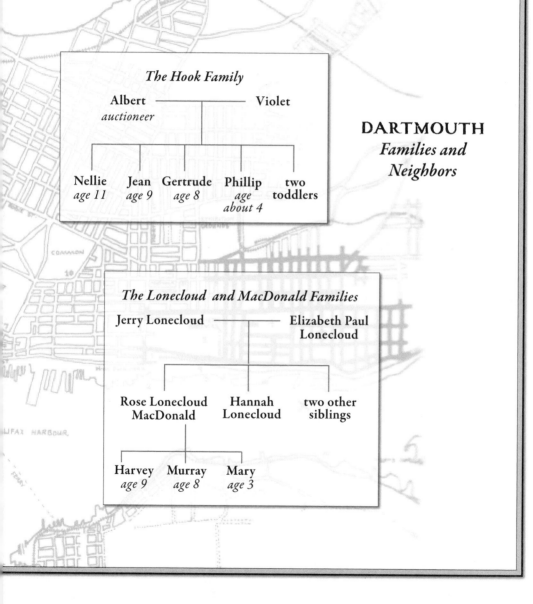

The Hook Family

Albert ——————— Violet
auctioneer

Nellie   Jean   Gertrude   Phillip   two
age 11   *age 9*   *age 8*   *age*   toddlers
                                      about 4

DARTMOUTH
Families and Neighbors

The Lonecloud and MacDonald Families

Jerry Lonecloud ——————— Elizabeth Paul
                                       Lonecloud

Rose Lonecloud   Hannah   two other
MacDonald   Lonecloud   siblings

Harvey   Murray   Mary
age 9   *age 8*   *age 3*

CONTENTS

NOTE TO THE READER

---∞∞∞---

AMERICANS AND CANADIANS spell certain words differently—for example, *color* versus *colour* and *harbor* versus *harbour*. Over time, Americans dropped the *u* when spelling both of these words. In the text, when referring in general to the body of water where this story takes place, I use the American spelling, *harbor*. But the proper name of that harbor, which is in Canada, is Halifax Harbour. When mentioning it by its full name, I use the Canadian spelling.

The treasuries of Canada and the United States call their paper currency by the same name—dollars. However, a Canadian dollar is not usually the exact cash equivalent of a U.S. dollar. In this book, all dollar amounts are given in Canadian dollars unless specified as U.S. dollars. In either case, the currency amounts are as they appear in the documents of the time and are not converted into modern-day equivalents.

As the cities in this story grew, some streets were renamed. In Halifax today, Barrington Street runs along the waterfront for most of the north–south length of the city. But until the beginning of 1917, the portion of Barrington Street that ran through the Richmond neighborhood, where much of this story occurs, was named Campbell Road. For longtime residents, getting used to the name change wasn't

ix

easy. Out of habit, many of the survivors, when talking about their experiences during the explosion and its aftermath, referred to the street by its old name. And of course it was listed as Campbell Road on old maps. To avoid confusion, I have used Barrington Street, its official name by December 1917.

In 1917, the Mi'kmaq (pronounced *MEE-gamok* and often spelled as "Micmac" in historical documents) settlement in the Halifax area was in a district of Dartmouth called Turtle Grove, which is located just south of an area called Tufts Cove. Depending on the source, the settlement is called either the Tufts Cove Mi'kmaq settlement or the Turtle Grove Mi'kmaq settlement. After canvassing many people and receiving mixed answers, I have chosen to use Tufts Cove. This is the name that Jeremiah (Jerry) Lonecloud, one of the elders who lived in the Mi'kmaq settlement, used in his letters written in 1917 to the Department of Indian Affairs.

In keeping with long-established seafaring tradition, I refer to a ship as "she" or "her."

It's against our nature not to know about times past.
We need stories. We need stories the way we need bread or water.
—David McCullough,
AUTHOR AND HISTORIAN

❧❦

A STORY TO TELL

HALIFAX, THE LARGEST CITY OF Nova Scotia, Canada, has a story to tell. Fourteen bells in a memorial tower ring part of the tale. In the city hall clock tower, the locked-in-place hands on the clock that faces north freeze a moment of the story, left as it was on that long-ago day. A museum containing grim reminders and libraries filled with age-old pages share more. The people of Halifax add chapters

to the story each time they speak the memories of those who lived—and died—at that time. Old scars are hidden by sturdy stone houses, and tall trees line remade streets. But the roots of the story are still there, and they grow deep.

The hands of this clock always remain at 9:05, a silent remembrance of a terrible tragedy. [Sally M. Walker]

Located on a small peninsula surrounded by salty water, Halifax is rich with history. People have lived in the area for ten thousand years. "Since time out of mind," the settlements

One of the birch-bark-covered dwellings in the Mi'kmaq settlement at Tufts Cove in about 1900.
[Nova Scotia Archives and Records Management]

and campsites of the Mi'kmaq, members of Canada's First Nations people, have dotted the landscape. Generation after generation, men and boys hunted in the evergreen forests; they fished in the lakes and flowing rivers. Women and girls built sturdy birch-bark-covered wigwams and gathered plants for food and medicinal use. They stitched clothing and made baskets decorated with elaborate patterns of interwoven porcupine quills. For hundreds of years, the Mi'kmaq found the rocky shore along Halifax's large, hourglass-shaped harbor a perfect place to live.

In the early 1600s, French explorers reached the shores of Nova Scotia and called the land Acadia. The Mi'kmaq allowed them to establish settlements where fishers dried their catches before shipping them to Europe. By the 1620s, Scottish settlers had made their way to the land, calling it Nova Scotia, which means "New Scotland" in Latin. For the next century, Great Britain and France played tug-of-war over Nova Scotia. Great Britain was the eventual victor.

In 1749, under the leadership of Edward Cornwallis, ships carrying more than 2,500 British settlers arrived and established a town they named Halifax. It became the capital of Nova Scotia, the leading port city for eastern Canada, and the site of a naval base. The Mi'kmaq, still living on most of their traditional lands, signed peace treaties with the British. In the late 1700s, an earthen fort named Fort Needham was constructed on the top of a 220-foot hill that overlooked the dockyards along the northern end of the city. In 1828, a stone fort called the Citadel was built on an even higher hill nearby. And all around the two hills, people built homes, schools, and businesses. Merchant ships sailed in and out of Halifax Harbour. By the 1860s, trains chugged into the city. Together, the railroad and ships created a transportation network that carried timber and fish and other trade goods to places around the world. And so Halifax grew.

By 1914, the population of Halifax had swelled to over 45,000 people. But it wasn't the only thriving town in the area. Across the harbor, more than 6,500 people, including a small settlement of Mi'kmaq, lived in the city of Dartmouth. There, an oil refinery as well as companies that produced goods such as ice skates, rope, beer, and chocolate provided

jobs for the area residents. While many of them knew there was political unrest in Europe—there was even talk of a war—it seemed unlikely that it would affect them, being so far away. During the summer of 1914, however, shattering events in Europe began a deathly trail that eventually found its way to Halifax and Dartmouth.

As countries in Europe began challenging each other for control of territory, they amassed armies that grew ever larger. Suspicions and mistrust escalated to a fever pitch as countries formed alliances with one another. An alliance is an agreement between different countries that joins them together for a purpose, often to wage war. By joining forces, allied countries also have greater power to withstand an enemy army. In 1914, Great Britain, France, and Russia formed an alliance against Germany, Austria-Hungary (which at that time was one country), and Italy. And then, in June, Archduke Francis Ferdinand, the heir to the throne of

Austria-Hungary, was assassinated. The assassin was a man from Serbia, a country that was a longtime enemy of Austria-Hungary.

Enraged by the killing, the government of Austria-Hungary declared war against Serbia. The action was supported by Germany, its ally. Invasions of territory and further declarations of war followed as Austria-Hungary and Germany challenged the allied governments of Great Britain, France, and Russia. By the end of August 1914, Europe had plunged into the four-year maelstrom of death and destruction that became known as World War I. Since it was then a colony of Great Britain, Canada entered the war at this time, too.

Because of its thriving port and deep harbor, Halifax became a major "jumping-off" point for ships carrying troops and supplies from North America to war-torn countries across the Atlantic. Three years later, it became even busier after the United States declared war on Germany on April 6, 1917, and entered into the alliance that included Great Britain. By the first week in December 1917, Halifax was bursting at the seams. Ships of all sizes, many of them from the United States, floated in Halifax Harbour. More than five thousand Canadian soldiers, some of whom brought their families with them, flooded the city. The housing crunch was incredible: Rooming houses, apartments, and private homes were packed, perhaps no area more so than the Richmond neighborhood, at the north end of Halifax.

Richmond, built around the steep flanks of Fort

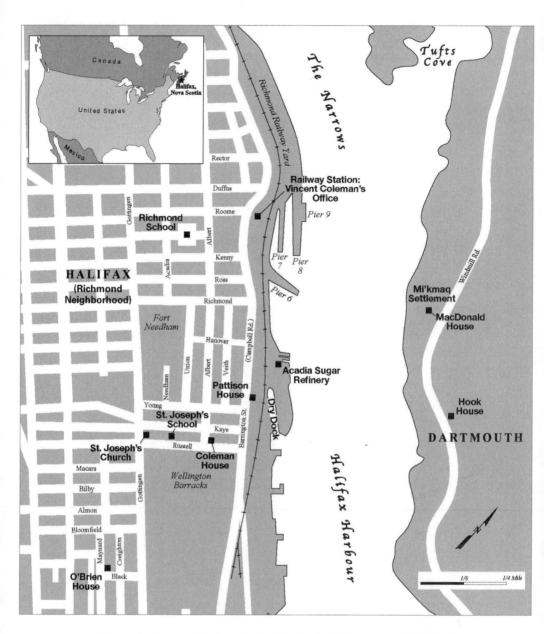

Houses, businesses, schools, and churches lined the busy streets of Halifax's Richmond neighborhood. [Map adapted by Len Walther from "Plan of the City of Halifax," Nova Scotia Archives and Records Management V6/240 c. (1910)]

Needham, was a bustling place. Yet even though thousands of people lived there, the neighborhood still held reminders of country life. In many backyards, hens clucked in chicken coops. Pigs snuffled inside sheds. Cows chewed their cud in backyard barns. And certain businessmen, such as milkmen or wagoners, owned horses to pull their vehicles. Many of the dwellings were single-family homes. There were also row houses—homes connected to one another—with several apartments in each. Most of the dwellings were made of wood. Only some of them had electricity. Many had indoor bathrooms that included a toilet, but some did not.

An electric tram trundled on a track on Barrington Street, which ran north and south along the waterfront.

People in Richmond often rode the electric tram that ran on tracks along Barrington Street.
[Nova Scotia Archives and Records Management]

Horse-drawn wagons rumbled over dirt and cobblestone streets. Automobiles and trucks were becoming more frequent, but most families in Richmond did not own a car—they simply could not afford it. Although concrete sidewalks were on a few streets near businesses, they were a rarity elsewhere in the north end of Halifax.

Richmond was largely a working-class neighborhood. The dockyard, shipping companies, and railroad employed thousands of people. Several factories produced goods such as cotton fabrics, flour, newspapers, beer, and metalwork, all of which provided steady work for the city's residents.

The Acadia Sugar Refinery was the tallest building on Richmond's waterfront. [Nova Scotia Archives and Records Management]

Many men were employed at the Acadia Sugar Refinery. Among other businesses, the shops in Richmond included groceries, pharmacies, furniture and shoe stores, and at least one laundry. At that time, most married women worked in their homes, caring for their children and keeping house—a full-time job with few, if any, of today's labor-saving devices. And of course Richmond's children went to school.

The war in Europe cast a pall on the autumn season. The newspapers carried stories of battles and listed names of the dead on a daily basis. Many families had a father or a son who was fighting overseas. Wounded soldiers in the military hospitals were a constant reminder of the dangers their loved ones faced. Even so, as December arrived, many people in Halifax and Dartmouth looked toward the holiday season with hope and excitement, thinking about the good times in store for them and what gifts they planned to make and give. Probably none of them knew about two ships named *Imo* and *Mont-Blanc*, each one making its way across the Atlantic Ocean. And if they had, they probably wouldn't have given them a second thought; ships were commonplace in Halifax Harbour. No one had the slightest inkling that these two ships would create the most terrible chapter in the two cities' story—one that would change lives forever.

❧2❧

STEAMING TOWARD DISASTER
NOVEMBER 25 TO DECEMBER 5

AFTER CROSSING THE ATLANTIC OCEAN, *Mont-Blanc*'s gleaming light-gray hull entered the Gravesend dockyard in Brooklyn, New York, on November 25, 1917. The 320-foot-long *Mont-Blanc* was not a stranger to North American shores. First launched as a freighter in England in 1899, she was later sold to Compagnie Générale Transatlantique, a French company. By 1917, *Mont-Blanc* had traveled to and from America several times.

Because of the war raging in Europe, the allied forces needed ships, lots of them, to carry supplies to the troops in a timely fashion. To meet this demand, the French Admiralty—the division of France's government that controlled the country's navy—placed all large French merchant ships under its command during the years 1914 to 1918. The Admiralty ordered *Mont-Blanc* to North America, where she would be refitted, or remodeled, so she could carry much-needed cargo back to France.

For this trip, *Mont-Blanc* had a new commander, Captain

Aimé Le Médec. Although he had never sailed on *Mont-Blanc* before, Le Médec was a seaman with more than sixteen years of experience. During two of those years, he had served as the captain on other ships. He had a reputation as a stern but fair commander with an accident-free career. As long as they didn't encounter any German U-boats (submarines), Le Médec expected that he and his crew would steer the 3,121-ton *Mont-Blanc*—and the cargo she was sent to collect—safely back to France.

During the last week in November, the forty men who crewed *Mont-Blanc* watched her being refitted. It wasn't long before they suspected their cargo was something out of the ordinary. Two large guns were installed on deck, one fore

Mont-Blanc *had made several trips to the United States before 1917.* [Maritime Museum of the Atlantic]

and one aft. By itself, that would not be unusual, considering the war. But then they noticed that the shipwrights, people who build ships, were installing wooden linings that completely covered the iron walls of *Mont-Blanc*'s four holds, the compartments in a ship's hull. Next, they probably noticed that the shipwrights secured the linings with nails made of copper, rather than iron. Copper is a metal that doesn't create sparks if it is struck with a sharp blow from another piece of metal. The crew's suspicions about the nature of the cargo grew further when the hold covers and the batten bars that held them in place were also covered with wood. By then it was understood that *Mont-Blanc*'s new cargo was something dangerous.

Any lingering doubts vanished when the stevedores, workers responsible for loading and unloading a ship's cargo, wrapped their shoes with linen cloth before carrying the cargo on board. This was highly unusual and would only have been done to prevent the metal nails in the bottoms of their shoes from creating sparks as they trekked across the metal deck. It was clear to all that *Mont-Blanc* was being loaded with explosives.

For more than a day, stevedores stuffed *Mont-Blanc*'s four holds with barrels, kegs, and cases containing picric acid, trinitrotoluene (often called TNT), and a substance called gun cotton. All of these materials are explosives. And there was more. Metal drums, stacked three to four high and filled with a flammable chemical called benzene, lined *Mont-Blanc*'s deck. By the time she was loaded, *Mont-Blanc* was a monstrously large bomb packed with 2,925 tons of explosive materials—a truly deadly cargo.

The weight of the cargo, plus the weight of more than a million pounds of coal needed to power *Mont-Blanc*'s steam engine, slowed the ship's speed so much that she would be unable to keep up with a convoy of ships crossing back to Europe from New York. Recognizing that traveling with a convoy would give *Mont-Blanc* the best protection from German U-boats, harbor authorities advised Le Médec to travel up the coast to Halifax, Nova Scotia. Larger convoys, arranged by Canada's Royal Navy, departed from Halifax's protected harbor. Perhaps one of them could accommodate the slow-moving *Mont-Blanc*. If not, the authorities in Halifax could give Le Médec instructions on the safest routes across the Atlantic. At 11:00 P.M. on December 1, Le Médec gave orders to cast off. The temperature was about 37 degrees Fahrenheit, fairly mild for that time of year, and the weather was fair. Le Médec looked forward to smooth sailing and an uneventful four-day trip to Halifax.

IN BEDFORD BASIN

On December 3, as *Mont-Blanc* chugged her way toward Nova Scotia, another large ship, named *Imo*, had just dropped anchor in Bedford Basin, the bay that forms the northernmost part of Halifax Harbour. Ships enter and exit the Bedford Basin through the Narrows, a strait between the cities of Halifax and Dartmouth. At its narrowest, the passage is less than 500 yards across. To avoid collisions, large ships such as

Imo required the navigation skills of experienced harbor pilots who were familiar with the harbor basin.

Imo was built in 1889, in Belfast, Ireland. Before the war, she had been used as a cargo liner and also to carry livestock such as horses. She was registered as a Norwegian ship, and at 430 feet long, was much longer than *Mont-Blanc*. Unlike *Mont-Blanc*, *Imo* was not carrying munitions—war supplies such as weapons. She was owned by the South Pacific Whaling Company and was under charter, a leaselike agreement, to the Belgian Relief Commission. (The country of Belgium declared itself neutral during World War I, but German troops occupied land in Belgium for much of the war.) As a neutral ship, *Imo* delivered aid, such as food, to people in war-ravaged Belgium. She had left Rotterdam, in the Netherlands, and steamed to Halifax.

After refueling, her commander, Captain Haakon From, and her thirty-nine-member crew were scheduled to go to New York, where the ship would be loaded with relief materials. Two large white signs, one on each side of *Imo*'s hull, bore the words BELGIAN RELIEF in large red letters. This notified other ships that she was not a warship and should be left alone. (By this time in the war, German ships had begun capturing relief vessels, but they were still labeled as such with the hope that they would not be attacked.)

With his ship anchored in Bedford Basin on the afternoon of December 5, Captain From watched the clock as coal was dumped into *Imo*'s hold. He had been a ship captain for more than ten years. He had been to Halifax on other trips and was familiar with the harbor routine. He knew that only harbor pilots from Halifax were permitted to direct ships in and out of the harbor. Harbor pilot William Hayes, an experienced pilot with a good reputation, had been assigned to steer *Imo* out of the harbor. Captain From also knew that, although he had already received permission to leave the harbor, if the coal delivery wasn't completed before late afternoon, *Imo* would have to spend another night in Bedford Basin. This was a non-negotiable wartime safety regulation.

Because German U-boats cruised the north Atlantic near Halifax, two antisubmarine nets made of steel mesh had been set in place across the harbor. The outer net extended from the tip of the Halifax peninsula to McNabs Island in the harbor; farther up the harbor, the inner net extended from the

Ships often docked at Pier 6, in Richmond. The Narrows section of the harbor is visible behind the masts of the ship docked at the pier. [Nova Scotia Archives and Records Management]

The wire-mesh submarine nets that stretched across the harbor were held in place by large, round floats. [Nova Scotia Archives and Records Management]

north and south ends of Georges Island to the Halifax and Dartmouth shores. Concrete weights attached to the bottom of the mesh held the nets in place on the harbor floor. Large, round floats at the surface kept the nets upright in the water. Gates in the nets were opened during the day to allow ships to enter and leave the harbor. But each day, shortly before dark, the gates were drawn shut—a sturdy barrier to enemy vessels that might try to sneak into the harbor under the cover of darkness. Captain From hoped the coal sliding into *Imo*'s hull would be loaded before the gates were shut for the night.

NIGHT FALLS

At the same time men were loading coal into *Imo*'s hold, *Mont-Blanc* arrived at the mouth of Halifax Harbour. Harbor pilot Francis Mackey boarded her and introduced himself to Captain Le Médec. Like Le Médec's spotless career, Mackey's twenty-four years of accident-free service seemed especially suited to *Mont-Blanc*, given her dangerous cargo. Although Mackey did not speak any French and Le Médec's English was limited, the two men were able to communicate with each other by using standard ship's terms—such as *port*, which means "left," and *starboard*, which means "right."

As dusk approached, a boat pulled alongside *Mont-Blanc*. On board was an examining officer whose job was to check what kind of cargo a ship carried and to supply the ship with orders for travel into the harbor. One of the men from the examiner's boat boarded *Mont-Blanc*. Pilot Mackey told him that they were standing above tons of TNT and picric acid and that the deck was loaded with benzene. He warned the man, "That's a . . . bad cargo," and continued the discussion saying, "Tell the examining officer . . . that I expect to get special orders for this ship. . . . Ask him if he can arrange it."

By the time the inspection of *Mont-Blanc*'s cargo papers had been completed, it was after 5:00 P.M. and the harbor gates had already been closed. The examining officer told Mackey and Le Médec that *Mont-Blanc* would have to wait until morning to enter the harbor. He then passed the news to his commanding officer that *Mont-Blanc* was carrying explosives and was waiting to enter. Hoping for an early start the next morning, Mackey accepted Le Médec's invitation to spend the night on board *Mont-Blanc*.

Up in Bedford Basin, the last of the coal was loaded into

❧ 3 ❧

DECEMBER 6, 1917

WHEN THE SUN ROSE ON THURSDAY, December 6, the sky was clear and blue. The air was crisp but not freezing cold. A light mist clung to the surface of Halifax Harbour, but it would disappear when the sun rose higher. A smudgy haze, thick with the scent of burning coal, wafted from the chimneys of Halifax and Dartmouth. Both cities bustled with morning activity. People on early work shifts had already started their days. The ferries were filled with commuters crossing the harbor. Shopkeepers prepared to open their doors, horse-drawn wagons rumbled down the roads, and women cooked breakfast for their children, many of whom were buttoning their shoes to get ready for school.

THE HOOK FAMILY

Albert Hook, a well-known auctioneer, lived with his family in a wooden house on Windmill Road, just north of downtown Dartmouth. That morning, at about eight o'clock, Mr. Hook had left home to catch the north-end ferry for his morning ride to Halifax. His wife, Violet, and the family's youngest children were at home in their large, L-shaped kitchen. Eight-year-old Gertrude and three of her younger siblings, including her brother Phillip, were eating breakfast. Her two older sisters, Nellie and Jean, were already in school, since classes for the older students started earlier than Gertrude's did. But Gertrude knew she had to finish eating soon. Even though she lived only a few blocks from Victoria School, the two-room schoolhouse where she attended third grade, they were long blocks. Maybe if she left early enough, she would have time to run and peek in the window of the candy store across the street from her house.

THE LONECLOUD AND MACDONALD FAMILIES

In another area of Dartmouth, a short distance from Gertrude's house, Mi'kmaq children were also thinking about going to school. The Tufts Cove Mi'kmaq community was located in the heart of the Narrows, on a section of land between the spruce woods and the rocky Dartmouth shoreline. During the years 1912 to 1917, between sixteen and twenty families lived in the neighborhood formed by a cluster of seven small wooden homes. Some of the men worked as laborers in Dartmouth businesses such as the Imperial Oil Company. Others earned income by cutting wood and fashioning it into ax handles, hockey sticks, and snowshoes. Like their ancestors, the women continued to weave baskets and other items, including boxes and purses, which they decorated with porcupine quills or beads. These items were very popular with tourists, who bought them at the market in Halifax, at railroad stations, and at the resorts that dotted the Dartmouth shoreline.

Jerry Lonecloud and his wife, Elizabeth, were well-known residents of the Tufts Cove community. In the late 1800s, the couple had traveled widely in the United States, where they had been performers in a Wild West show. Upon their return to Nova Scotia in the 1890s, Lonecloud became highly respected for his knowledge of herbal medicines and traditional Mi'kmaq culture and as a storyteller of Mi'kmaq legends. In his role as a community leader, he tirelessly advocated with the Department of Indian Affairs on behalf of the Mi'kmaq and their right to occupy land in the Dartmouth area—a right that was disputed by some white people. In fact, just that autumn the Department of Indian Affairs had agreed to buy 94½ acres of nearby land from a local family to establish a permanent reservation for the Tufts Cove Mi'kmaq. An order to relocate the Mi'kmaq families to this property had been issued on November 6, 1917. But as of December, the relocation of the Loneclouds and other Tufts Cove families had not yet occurred. Although Lonecloud agreed to eventually move his family to a reservation about 35 miles from Halifax, he believed none of the Mi'kmaq should leave Tufts Cove without being fairly paid for the land they had occupied for so long.

On the morning of December 6, Jerry, Elizabeth, and the two youngest Lonecloud children were away from Tufts Cove. Their teenage daughter Hannah remained behind with her sister Rose Lonecloud MacDonald and Rose's

Rose Lonecloud MacDonald with one of her three children. [Maritime Museum of the Atlantic]

three children, who also lived in Tufts Cove.

Rose's nine-year-old son, Harvey, was sick with the flu. He watched his mother comb her long black hair back into a bun. She bustled about the kitchen, stoking the coals in the stove as she prepared breakfast. She constantly warned three-year-old Mary to keep away from the stove. Harvey hated being sick and staying in bed. He much preferred being outside, doing something like ice skating. Or, if his grandfather Jerry Lonecloud had been home, maybe they could have gone fishing or hunting. Already, Harvey was a good marksman, and he was proud that he could make a moose call from birch bark. And his loon imitation . . . well, he had just about perfected the waterbird's loud, whinny-like scream. But he couldn't do any of that inside, in bed. His mother, gentle as she was, didn't appreciate loud loon noises in the house. Besides, it was a school day. If he'd been well, his mother would have been telling him to get ready for school.

While Harvey rested in bed, he watched his eight-year-old brother, Murray, get dressed. The MacDonald boys attended the nearby Indian School along with the other Mi'kmaq children. Because they were denied attendance at the public school, the Mi'kmaq residents had established their own school in 1913, in a building donated by William Nevins, a member of the Mi'kmaq community. They hired George Richardson, from Halifax, as the school's principal and only teacher. In fact, while Murray MacDonald was getting ready for school, Richardson, who lived across the harbor in the Richmond neighborhood, had already started his day, leaving plenty of time for his morning commute by ferry to the Indian School across the harbor.

WELCOME TO THE STREETS OF RICHMOND

Like the people in Dartmouth, residents of Halifax's Richmond neighborhood were also busy starting their day. Machines thrummed in the cotton factory, men unloaded boxes from railroad cars, and stevedores carried them onto ships. Milkmen drove their wagons from house to house, stopping to deliver orders for milk and cream. Shopkeepers opened the doors of their establishments, and children left for school.

Jerry Lonecloud made this birch-bark moose call in 1915. His grandson Harvey enjoyed making these calls too. [Sally M. Walker]

THE PATTISON FAMILY

As the minutes ticked toward eight-thirty, Vincent Pattison, an engineer at the Acadia Sugar Refinery, had already been at work for some time. He'd arrived early—aided by the borrowed pocket watch he carried while his own watch was in the shop for repairs. Mr. Pattison didn't like to be late, so he deliberately turned the minute hand of the watch ahead a few minutes, ensuring that he would always be on time. Located on the harbor's edge, the sugar refinery and its

Vincent Pattison and his family pose for a snapshot on the porch of their home. In the front row (from left to right) are Alan, Vincent, Katharine, James, and Gordon; the two women standing in back are Georgina Grant (left) and her sister Annie Pattison.
[Maritime Museum of the Atlantic]

smokestack loomed several stories higher than the Richmond homes nearby.

While Mr. Pattison was busy at the refinery, his wife, Annie, was equally busy in their wooden house on Barrington Street. Several weeks earlier, the company had finally persuaded Mr. Pattison to move his family from Gottingen Street, which was farther from the waterfront, to the company-owned house on Barrington. The street was a busy one, especially with the tram tracks out front, but it was closer to his job. And Mumford's Drugstore was only a few

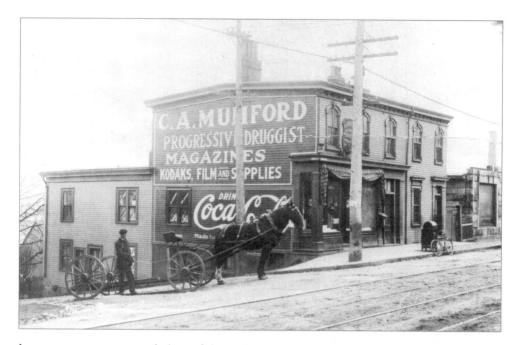

houses away—nice and close if there was money to spare for a soda or a piece of candy.

Like many children that week, Katharine, the Pattisons' eleven-year-old daughter, was sick with a cold. Mrs. Pattison decided that Katharine needed a day at home to recuperate. Still, she had a lively bunch of three other children to feed and get ready for school. At fourteen, thirteen, and nine, the Pattison boys, Gordon, James, and Alan, were a flurry of activity. Gordon, the oldest, was the boisterous one of the bunch; he was the risk taker, always ready for a dare. When Halifax Harbour froze, he loved to grab his ice skates and zip over to Georges Island—the same island where one end of the submarine net had been placed. When a church was being built near his grandparents' home in the area of Dartmouth called Woodside, it was Gordon who climbed the scaffolding.

Everyone in the neighborhood knew Mumford's Drugstore. On snowy winter days, people with horse-pulled sledges like this one replaced the wheels with runners.
[Nova Scotia Archives and Records Management]

[LEFT] *Without a bathing costume, Katharine Pattison had to settle for wading with her brothers in the harbor.* [Courtesy of Grant Pattison]

[RIGHT] *From left to right: James, Gordon, and Alan Pattison loved to swim, play games, and have fun.* [Nova Scotia Archives and Record Management]

Fearlessly, he scrambled right to the top, where the cross would be placed when the church was completed. James, only thirteen months younger, loved to play games and have fun, but he wasn't as daring as his brother. And as the "baby" of the family, Alan was happy when his big brothers let him tag along.

The Pattison children attended Richmond School, on Roome Street. Although classes didn't begin until nine-thirty, the boys planned to leave a few minutes before nine o'clock. They didn't want to be late—eight blocks was a long way to run if they were. For the past few weeks, Gordon and James had been very conscious of time. On their birthdays in September and October, each had received a watch as a gift. Both felt quite grown up, having their own timepieces. Gordon's had a fancy cover that protected the watch face, while James had a pocket watch. Earlier, Gordon had proudly

This is a photo of one of the classes at Richmond School. Katharine Pattison is in the second row, fifth student from the left. [Maritime Museum of the Atlantic]

strapped his new watch around his wrist. James didn't have his watch because his father had borrowed it that morning. But James was proud that his watch would help his dad. Besides, the boys were confident that Gordon's watch would keep them on schedule.

THE O'BRIEN FAMILY

There was no space to spare in Albert and Bertie O'Brien's home on Maynard Street. The O'Briens and their ten children lived in a five-room apartment in a house a few blocks from Wellington Barracks, where many of the soldiers stationed in Halifax lived. To make ends meet, Albert O'Brien had a couple of different jobs. In the daytime, he worked the early shift as a stevedore for the Furness Withy shipping company. In the evening, he worked as a lamplighter. Occasionally, his seven-year-old son, Gerald, accompanied him, watching his father light the gas lamps that brightened the city's streets at night.

Every penny counted in the O'Brien household. Gerald's oldest sister, twenty-one-year-old Evelyn, worked at Ungar's Laundry, where she earned $5.50 a week. (By comparison, a skilled laborer, such as a carpenter, earned about 40 cents an hour in 1917.) Evelyn's weekly wages provided money to buy much-needed groceries. At seventeen, Gerald's sister Laura should have been working, but that December she was frail and in poor health. Many teenagers, however, worked full-time as soon as they finished ninth grade. At that time, in order to attend high school, a student's family had to buy all the necessary books and supplies, something many Richmond families could not afford to do. Instead, a teenager was expected to find a job in a factory, at the dockyard, in a store, or at the railroad.

Even with the added income from Evelyn's job, the O'Briens were mindful of their money and took care not to lose it. Just that morning, before leaving the house, Mr. O'Brien had tucked a twice-folded five-dollar bill deep inside his wallet where it couldn't slip out. By the time his morning was well under way, he wasn't thinking about the five dollars any longer. He was hard at work hauling cargo down at the dry dock.

With so many mouths to feed, Mrs. O'Brien had quickly learned that soup as a meal was both filling and economical. That morning, she decided to add barley, a chewy grain similar to rice, to the soup she had simmering on the stove for dinner. Unfortunately, she'd run out of barley, so she asked Gerald to run to the store for her.

Unlike the Pattison boys, Gerald O'Brien wasn't thinking about hurrying to school. The boys' classes at St. Joseph's Catholic School didn't start until later in the day. Boys shared the school with girls, which seemed odd to Gerald. But St. Joseph's boys' school had burned down the previous year, and the new school wasn't ready yet. This year, all the children shared the same building: The girls attended school in the morning; the boys went in the afternoon. So Gerald knew he had plenty of time to walk to the store.

THE COLEMAN FAMILY

For slightly over two years, the Coleman family had lived in a house on Russell Street, at the corner where it intersected with Albert Street. Together in that neat, wooden home, Vincent Coleman and his wife, Frances, had grieved when their younger son, Cyril, died of diphtheria in 1915. The birth of Eileen, their third daughter, the next year helped bring laughter back into their lives. In December 1917, the Colemans were snug and happy in their home.

Vincent Coleman was a telegrapher for the Canadian Government Railways. He left early each morning and returned late at night. Fortunately, his home was just a few blocks—two of which were downhill—from the station. The hubbub of rolling railway cars and docking ships surrounded the office where Mr. Coleman worked. It was his job as a telegrapher to control the train traffic. He directed incoming rail cargo to the correct wharf for sea transport. He made sure that passengers and troops

From left to right: Eleanor, Cyril, Gerald, and Juanita Coleman, in 1915.
[Courtesy of Janette Snooks]

who needed to arrive at the nearby North Street station got there without any problem.

Two Coleman children, seven-year-old Eleanor and eleven-year-old Gerald, attended St. Joseph's Catholic School, a short walk from their home. Even though Gerald didn't have school in the morning, he planned to leave home with Eleanor. That morning he was serving as an altar boy in St. Joseph's Church. He would walk Eleanor to school and continue on to the church. Thirteen-year-old Juanita—Nita, to her family—was staying home from school with a painful case of strep throat. The Coleman house, like many in Richmond, did not have electricity. Every Saturday, it was Nita's job to clean the smudgy coat of soot that blackened the glass chimneys of the oil lamps the family used to light the house at night. It was a dirty job, but Nita was proud that her

Girls who attended St. Joseph's School wore white pinafores as a uniform. This picture, taken in 1916 or 1917, is of the second-grade class. [Maritime Museum of the Atlantic]

parents trusted her not to break the glass. Her father was a loving man, but he did expect his children to do their chores. Nita hoped she'd be feeling well by the weekend so she could get her job done properly.

Eileen Coleman was only a toddler in 1917, so she did not go to school with her brother and sisters.
[Maritime Museum of the Atlantic]

Mr. Coleman's wife, Frances, was an excellent seamstress. That morning, she dressed Eileen in a blue dress she'd made for her and carried the toddler into the kitchen. Eileen often sat and watched her mother tidy up after breakfast. Mrs. Coleman enjoyed talking with Eileen—Babe, as she called her—encouraging the little girl to babble and learn more words. Like many mothers in Halifax and Dartmouth, she was thinking about caring for her sick daughter, cleaning the house, mending clothes, and deciding what to serve for dinner later in the day. The ships coming and going in the harbor were not high on her list of concerns.

❖ 4 ❖

IN HALIFAX HARBOUR

EVEN THOUGH FRANCES COLEMAN may not have been thinking about ships, plenty of other people were. More than forty vessels—large ships and small boats—floated in Halifax Harbour. *Curaca* and *Calonne*, two of the larger ships, would soon be loaded with horses that would pull supply wagons or carry the cavalry troops fighting in Europe. The equally large *Picton*, which was docked at the Acadia Sugar Refinery wharf for repairs, was loaded with a more general, mixed cargo that included some munitions. There were tugboats, ferries, minesweepers, patrol ships, and schooners (large two-masted sailboats). There were even two submarines moored at one of the Halifax piers. In short, the harbor bustled with as much activity as the surrounding cities.

Aboard *Mont-Blanc*, at the mouth of the harbor, pilot Francis Mackey, mindful of the ship's dangerous cargo, asked the harbor official again "if there was any special orders in the way of protection" for the ship. He was told "no, sir." Mackey accepted this assurance, and the ship's crew readied her for entry into the harbor. *Mont-Blanc* waited her turn, allowing *Clara*, a boat from the United States that carried general cargo, to pass through the submarine gate first. At about 7:30 A.M., a signal light blinked a message to one of *Mont-Blanc*'s officers, indicating that he should raise *Mont-Blanc*'s identifying flag and begin the trip up the harbor and into Bedford Basin.

Mackey piloted *Mont-Blanc* through the submarine gate, traveling slowly toward the Dartmouth side of the harbor. He did this to comply with standard regulations created to avoid collisions at sea. This regulation required that a steamship traveling through narrow channels should always keep as close to the shoreline on the ship's starboard (right) side as was safe. This means that when two ships are in a channel and heading toward each other, each ship stays to its own right, thus preventing a collision. (Cars traveling in opposite lanes of a road in America pass each other in a similar way.)

Up in Bedford Basin, *Imo* was ready for departure. Captain From ordered her anchor raised, and shortly after 8:00 A.M., she was under steam, heading south. Her hull, empty of cargo, rode high in the water. In this condition, if she needed to reverse direction and go backward, it would be a slow maneuver since her propeller was so close to the surface. But reversing direction was not in Captain From's plans. He wanted to get to New York as soon as possible. As *Imo* made her way toward the Narrows, she was hidden from the view of ships farther south in the harbor by the hilly land of the

Richmond neighborhood. Pilot Hayes knew that harbor regulations required him to keep *Imo* closer to the Halifax shoreline; heading seaward, this was on *Imo*'s starboard side. What Hayes didn't realize was that *Mont-Blanc* was in the harbor. He hadn't been informed that she was incoming.

As *Imo* swung into the Narrows, Hayes saw the ship *Clara* chugging toward him through the Narrows, close to the Halifax shore. (According to the harbor's established shipping regulations, *Clara* should have been traveling closer to the Dartmouth shore.) He could also see the tugboat *Stella Maris* towing a barge and moving out into the harbor from one of the Halifax docks. For whatever reasons, Captain From and Pilot Hayes decided to steer *Imo* out of the paths of *Clara* and *Stella Maris* rather than insisting that those ships yield the right of way. Doing this meant that From and Hayes steered *Imo* toward its left, bringing it closer to the Dartmouth side of the Narrows. One of the ways that ships communicated with each other while in the harbor was through the use of certain patterns of whistle blasts. Hayes ordered *Imo*'s whistle blown in a signal to *Clara*'s captain. The signal indicated that *Imo* would move closer to the Dartmouth shore; *Clara* could stay in her present course.

By this time, *Mont-Blanc* was approaching the Narrows. Captain Le Médec and Pilot Mackey could see *Imo* heading toward Dartmouth on a path that, if maintained, would cause the two ships to collide. *Mont-Blanc*'s whistle signaled to *Imo* to move toward Halifax. As both ships entered the Narrows and Hayes spotted *Mont-Blanc*, the two ships' whistles blared signals, one after another, and that's when the confusion began. Neither seemed to interpret the other's signal correctly. As the distance between the ships closed, Mackey decided that the only way to avoid a collision was to turn *Mont-Blanc* hard to her left, toward Halifax. He hoped this would give *Imo* enough room to sail safely between *Mont-Blanc* and the Dartmouth shore.

At the same time, Hayes ordered *Imo* into reverse. Unfortunately, due to the lighter weight of her cargoless hull, *Imo* was riding high in the water, leaving her propeller even closer to the surface. The ship was unable to reverse direction rapidly. Instead, her bow swung toward *Mont-Blanc*. From that instant, a collision was unavoidable. Within moments, *Imo* crashed through *Mont-Blanc*'s hull at the waterline. Before *Imo*'s forward momentum stopped, her bow had penetrated about nine feet into the number-one hold—packed full of explosive materials—on *Mont-Blanc*'s starboard side. The impact ripped *Mont-Blanc*'s hull open from just above the waterline up to the ship's rail, which in that part of the boat was a distance of about 20 feet. Drums of benzene tumbled loose. As the barrels crashed down, they burst open, splashing the flammable chemical across *Mont-Blanc*'s deck.

The situation worsened when *Imo*'s engines finally engaged in reverse and she began to back away from *Mont-Blanc*. As she did so, the port anchor attached to *Imo*'s bow snagged the edge of one of the protective metal plates near *Mont-Blanc*'s hold. Sparks flew as the metals scraped each other. The anchor ripped off the metal plate with a final tug that slightly changed

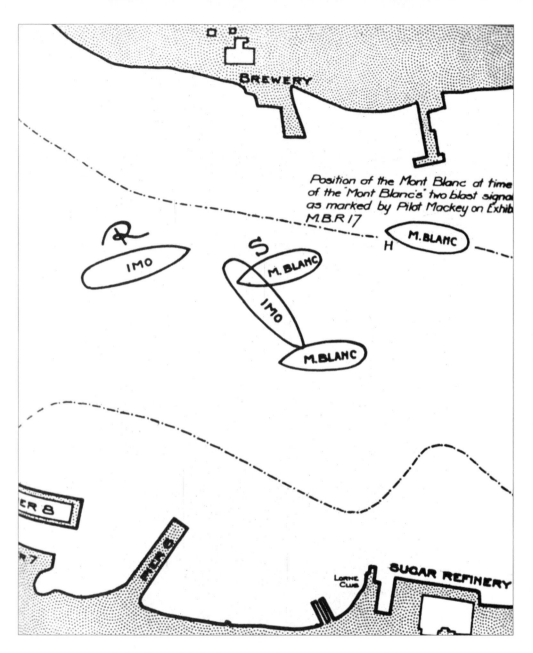

Position of the Mont Blanc at time
of the "Mont Blanc's" two blast signal
as marked by Pilot Mackey on Exhib
M.B.R 17

*According to Francis Mackey's testimony, later given in court and documented
in this diagram,* Mont-Blanc's *position changed, moving away from the
Dartmouth shore and into* Imo's *path.* [Maritime Museum of the Atlantic]

Mont-Blanc's course, causing her to head directly toward Richmond.

While the collision itself did not have enough force to explode *Mont-Blanc*'s entire cargo, some of the granules of explosive material in the hold were crushed during the collision. This triggered tiny flashes of fire that, in turn, ignited the benzene vapor. With a *whoosh*, larger flames quickly raced across the benzene-soaked deck.

In seconds, a roiling cloud of heavy black smoke billowed above *Mont-Blanc*. On deck, rapidly spreading flames cut off access to the ship's fire hose connection near the forward deck of the ship, and there were no fire extinguishers readily available. Inside the hold, as the fire spread and burned hotter, clouds of steam—created as harbor water that had flooded into the hull was vaporized by the heat—hissed from the large hole in the hull. It quickly became clear to Mackey and Captain Le Médec that *Mont-Blanc*'s crew would be unable to put out the fire. And there was not enough time to dismantle the ship's engines and purposely sink her, a process that would take hours. Knowing that an explosion was a certainty, Le Médec realized he had no choice but to lower the two lifeboats and abandon ship. After ensuring that his entire crew was in the lifeboats, Le Médec joined them.

Meanwhile, on board *Imo*, Captain From realized that his ship was not severely damaged. He ordered that she continue south, toward the mouth of the harbor, where she would have more room to turn around and head back for repair.

At the same time, *Mont-Blanc*'s crew frantically rowed their lifeboats toward the Dartmouth shore. Francis Mackey waved his arms and screamed out warnings, trying to alert nearby ships of the impending explosion. But his gestures went unseen, his shouts unheard.

ON THE WATERFRONT

Even though her engines had been turned off, *Mont-Blanc* still floated steadily toward shore, headed straight for Pier 6 in Richmond, growing more dangerous by the minute. It wasn't long before her pale gray hull, already blackened with carbon from the smoke, ran aground alongside Pier 6. Her hull actually touched the pier's timbers, causing them to ignite.

By this time, almost everyone in the area knew something unusual was happening. Many people grabbed their coats and ran toward the harbor, filling the streets as they tried to see the fire. Others made their way up to Fort Needham, where its crest offered a clear view of the burning ship. Hundreds more stopped whatever they were doing and stood at the windows of homes and office buildings, watching as orange and blue tongues of flame, many of which were two to three times higher than the tallest trees, streaked skyward inside the growing cloud. People shouted back and forth, adding to the commotion, as everyone tried to find out what was happening.

The harbor, too, was in an uproar. While the men on nearby ships did not know the nature of *Mont-Blanc*'s cargo, they could see that the situation was serious. Upon sighting

Imo in the Narrows, Horatio Brannen, captain of the tugboat *Stella Maris*, had turned his ship back toward the Halifax shore to avoid a collision. He had watched helplessly as *Mont-Blanc* and *Imo* collided. As soon as he realized *Mont-Blanc* was on fire and the burning ship had run aground, Brannen sprang into action, ordering his tugboat toward Pier 6. He hoped the fire hose on *Stella Maris* could pump enough water to extinguish the fire. If not, perhaps his tugboat could tow *Mont-Blanc* into deeper water, away from the piers and buildings crowded with people. Meanwhile, sailors from the British ship HMS *Highflyer* and from the Canadian Navy's ship HMCS *Niobe* lowered small boats with men from their crews who joined Brannen's men in trying to extinguish the fire.

❧ 5 ❧

SHORTLY BEFORE
NINE O'CLOCK

SHORTLY BEFORE NINE O'CLOCK, through the window of his grocery store, Constant Upham clearly saw *Mont-Blanc* burning beside the pier. Unlike most Richmond stores and homes, Upham's store had a telephone. Quickly, he rang the West End Fire House, where the Patricia, Halifax's only motorized fire pumper, was garaged. (At that time, the other fire engines in Halifax were still pulled by horses.) After reporting the blazing ship, Mr. Upham called more firehouses. In the West End Fire House, as the alarm bell clanged, driver Billy Wells climbed behind the Patricia's steering wheel. Within minutes, he and the rest of her crew were speeding toward the harbor.

As the Patricia raced along, Gordon, James, and Alan Pattison shouldered their book bags, thundered down the porch steps, and set out for Richmond School. They had scarcely walked a block when they heard the Patricia's siren. When they stopped to watch the pumper rush down the street, the boys noticed smoke rising above the rooftops between them and the dockyard. They had no idea what was on fire. Neither did Mrs. Pattison or their sister, Katharine, back at the house. But their father, Vincent Pattison, was inside the sugar factory next to Pier 6 and could, of course, see what was burning.

Shortly before nine o'clock, Gerald O'Brien clenched his fingers around the money his mother had given him, thinking, "Barley, barley, barley," so he wouldn't forget what to buy. As he skipped toward the store, he noticed people hurrying and shouting. He wondered what was happening. Gerald's father already knew. As Albert O'Brien moved boxes on board a ship that was in the dry dock for repairs, he could easily see the black cloud that rose above the sugar refinery tower and loomed like a wall between him and Pier 6.

Just beside Pier 6, Captain Brannen, his crew on the *Stella Maris*, and the men from *Highflyer* and *Niobe* realized they didn't have sufficient waterpower to extinguish *Mont-Blanc*'s fire. They began preparations to attach a hawser, or strong towing cable, to *Mont-Blanc*.

Shortly before nine o'clock, the two lifeboats carrying *Mont-Blanc*'s crew landed safely at Tufts Cove. The men climbed out and yelled at the onlookers to run for cover. Captain Le Médec and Pilot Mackey turned and, for a moment, watched the black cloud spread. Then Le Médec put his hand on Mackey's shoulder and said, "Go on, Mack, come on." They started to run for the woods.

While they ran, Hannah Lonecloud, also in Tufts Cove, stood outside with Rose MacDonald and Rose's son Murray, watching the ships and the smoke rising above the water. William Paul, a neighbor's boy, ran past them. He shouted that a white man near the wharf was yelling that a ship was going to explode. Not wanting to miss the action, Harvey got out of bed and joined his mother and brother outside. As soon as Rose saw Harvey, she ordered him to go inside the house and get back into bed.

At home, Gertrude Hook, still buttoning her coat, left the kitchen and started down the hall to the front door, forgetting her mittens in the kitchen. Gertrude's mother called out to her to come back for them.

Shortly before nine o'clock, the benzene-filled drums on *Mont-Blanc*'s deck began to explode one after another, flaring like fireworks inside the black cloud. Flashes turned the sky red and threw slivers and chunks of the metal drums, hot enough to glow, high into the air. Like a giant furnace burning wildly out of control, the fire grew increasingly hotter. Hot enough to evaporate the sweat from the skin of the men who fought the towering flames. Hot enough to evaporate the tears, caused by the acrid smoke, as they trickled down the cheeks of the people lining the piers and streets nearby. Hot enough to make the harbor water surrounding *Mont-Blanc*'s hull hiss, boil, and steam.

Shortly before nine o'clock, as the sky was turning an unusual shade of red, Eleanor Coleman and her classmates lined up in the schoolyard and filed down into the cloakroom in the basement of St. Joseph's School. Soon they would begin their morning prayers. Gerald Coleman and his friend Leo

Even as disaster loomed, Vincent Coleman remained at his desk to telegraph a warning. [Nova Scotia Archives and Records Management]

Fultz were in the sanctuary of St. Joseph's Church, preparing the altar for daily services. Frances, Juanita, and Eileen Coleman were still in the kitchen on Russell Street. Vincent Coleman sat at his telegraph dispatch station in the Richmond railway office, about 750 feet from Pier 6. By that time, unlike most of the people watching *Mont-Blanc* burn, Coleman knew that she was a munitions ship, that she carried explosives. He wanted to flee, but he was worried about the incoming trains—trains filled with people who were heading toward disaster if someone didn't stop them. And Mr. Coleman didn't want that to happen. Instead of leaving the office with his coworker, he turned back and reached for his telegraph key. He tapped out a final message, sending it to the Rockingham station five miles away: MUNITIONS SHIP ON FIRE IN THE HARBOUR. MAKING FOR PIER 6. GOODBYE.

AT 9:04 A.M.

Vincent Pattison, inside the sugar refinery, watched the *Mont-Blanc* burn.

On Barrington Street, his sons, Gordon, James, and Alan, ran toward the fire.

His wife, Annie, went into the backyard to see what was happening.

Katharine Pattison stayed inside the house.

Albert O'Brien stepped off the ship in the dry dock.

His son Gerald skipped toward the store.

At home, Albert's wife, Bertie, and his daughter Evelyn watched smoke fill the sky.

Vincent Coleman, his warning telegraph message sent, started to run.

At home, his wife, Frances, and daughters Juanita and Eileen heard sirens.

In school, Eleanor Coleman headed toward her classroom.

Gerald Coleman finished lighting candles in St. Joseph's Church.

On the waterfront, driver Billy Wells tightly gripped the *Patricia's* steering wheel.

In the harbor, Horatio Brannen and other seamen continued their rescue efforts.

Across the harbor, Rose MacDonald and her son Murray watched the black smoke spread.

Her sister, Hannah Lonecloud, stood nearby.

Little Mary peeked from the doorway of the house.

Rose's son Harvey, following her order, climbed back into bed.

Gertrude Hook, following *her* mother's order, turned back to get her mittens.

Pilot Francis Mackey and Captain Aimé Le Médec ran into the nearby woods.

Thirty seconds later, *Mont-Blanc*'s main cargo exploded.

Within seconds of the explosion, an enormous cloud filled the sky with thick, heavy smoke. [Library of Congress, Prints & Photographs Division reproduction #165-WW-158A-15]

✠ 6 ✠

A HORRENDOUS EXPLOSION

WHEN *IMO* AND *MONT-BLANC* COLLIDED, the impact of the collision had not detonated the explosives in *Mont-Blanc's* holds. But the repeated shocks that occurred as metal drums exploded on the deck crushed picric acid crystals and seriously jarred the TNT packed in the ship's holds. High explosives—such as picric acid and TNT—detonate under this kind of treatment, when the chemical bonds between the molecules of the explosive material are ripped apart. As the bonds break, they release energy, lots and lots of it, in a ferociously hot blast of gases called a shock wave. A shock wave races outward from the center of an explosion in the form of an enormous wave of pressure that is created when air molecules are pushed away from the blast site at supersonic speeds. When *Mont-Blanc's* cargo exploded, it was the largest manmade explosion that had ever occurred. It remained so until August 6, 1945, when the atom bomb was dropped on Hiroshima, Japan, during World War II.

Alan Ruffman and David Simpson, two scientists who later studied the explosive power of *Mont-Blanc*'s cargo, estimated that the temperature at the center of the explosion was about 9,032 degrees Fahrenheit—more than three times hotter than the temperature needed to melt iron. The initial speed of the shock wave as it traveled out from the explosive cargo was about 5,000 feet per second—nearly five times faster than sound travels through air. No one could outrun the supersonic blast.

As it did with the city hall clock tower, the shock of the blast stopped the hands on this clock, which was found among the ruins of a house in Richmond. [Maritime Museum of the Atlantic]

DEVASTATION

In less than the amount of time it takes to blink your eye, the shock wave had pushed across the piers and the railroad tracks. *Mont-Blanc*'s hull shattered into pieces that rained down across Halifax, the harbor, and Dartmouth. In another blink, the shock wave had traveled up and over Fort Needham, some of its force deflected upward by the hill, which offered a small measure of protection to the homes behind it. The wave traveled around the northern bend of Barrington Street, toward the African-Canadian neighborhood of Africville, its force again partially deflected by the base of the hill. Simultaneously, the shock wave spread across the harbor and up into Dartmouth.

In Halifax, the Richmond neighborhood received the blast's full force, as did Tufts Cove, across the Narrows, in Dartmouth. The fierce, unsparing power of the shock wave devastated both neighborhoods. In Halifax, every building inside the rectangle formed by Young Street, Fort Needham, Rector Street, and the harbor was completely destroyed. The blast splintered wooden homes, turning them into piles that looked like jumbled matchsticks. Roofs caved in as the stories below them collapsed. Stoves tipped over and spilled burning coals among the wreckage. Brick factories crumbled into mounds of rubble. The Acadia Sugar

In seconds, hundreds of homes were reduced to piles of broken boards.
[Maritime Museum of the Atlantic]

Refinery all but disappeared. The Richmond Printing Plant and the Hillis Foundry were transformed into eerie brick skeletons. Pier 6 completely vanished. All of Richmond's churches and an orphanage were destroyed. Richmond School, which the Pattison children attended, was in ruins. So was St. Joseph's School, where the Coleman children had been ready to start classes. All the buildings—twelve thousand of them—within a 16-mile radius were damaged in some way.

The shock wave snapped telegraph poles and trees in two as easily as if they'd been twigs. Electric wires, torn free and broken, sizzled and sparked on the ground. Train cars toppled off the rails, wagons overturned, and the horses that had pulled them lay dead in their harnesses. The wave cracked the hulls of ships and smashed the decks with flying debris. In Dartmouth, the rope factory and beer brewery were little more than piles of brick. Throughout both cities, the windows in homes and stores and offices and schools shattered in a deadly blizzard of glass. At the Halifax School for the Deaf, which had as many as four hundred windowpanes, Mr. Fearon, the principal, reported that "not a piece of glass as large as your hand was left intact . . . the floors were covered an inch deep with fragments."

The sound of the explosion depended on the location of the people who heard it. Some people in Halifax described it as a loud boom. Some said it was a terrible roar. Standing outside her home in Tufts Cove, Mrs. Paul reported that the explosion sounded like a loud buzz. (It was her son William who had shouted to his neighbors in the Mi'kmaq settlement that a ship was going to explode.) Still others, a few miles away, heard two explosions, which was puzzling because there was only a single large one. According to Alan Ruffman, the reason some people heard two sounds was because an energy wave like this does not only travel through the air; it also travels through the ground. And this kind of wave moves faster through rock than it does in air. Those who heard two explosions first heard the thump caused by vibrations that had raced ahead inside the rock. The second sound was actually the noise created by the same blast. It just arrived a few seconds later because the sound of the energy wave traveled slower through the air.

In Shubenacadie, a town about 40 miles from Halifax, people heard a low rumbling that gradually faded. The shock of the explosion broke windows 50 miles away, and people in Sydney, a town about 250 miles from Halifax, felt the ground shake.

An enormous cloud of smoke, gray at first and then fading to white, spewed skyward. Because the winds were light that morning, the cloud reached a height of more than 11,000 feet. It hung there in the terrible stillness that followed the explosion until air currents high in the atmosphere gradually pushed the top of the cloud toward the southeast. At sea, 50 miles from Halifax, men aboard the USS *Tacoma* saw the cloud on the horizon. Recognizing that a cloud that large must have been caused by a dreadful explosion, they changed course and headed for the harbor.

BLACK RAIN AND A GIANT WAVE

As devastating as the destruction already was, more was yet to come as the outward-spreading shock wave gradually dissipated. During the initial blast, the tremendous pressure of the shock wave so completely pushed air molecules away from the blast site that it created an almost airless condition, like a vacuum, in the area surrounding the explosion site. Unless air is prevented from doing so, it always flows into a

Richmond School (sometimes called Roome Street School) lay in ruins. Although only two children were killed inside the building when it collapsed, eighty-seven of the students died in the explosion. [Maritime Museum of the Atlantic]

vacuum. So, as soon as the outward movement of the air wave slowed, a new gust of air rushed back to fill the partial vacuum around the explosion site. The force of this second gust was so strong that it further damaged any buildings still standing.

Then for ten minutes the gigantic cloud pelted the devastated areas with a black rain made thick with benzene residue. The slick liquid coated everything and everyone with greasy soot that penetrated clothing and stained people's skin black. Along with the oily rain, debris, including boulders and broken pieces of *Mont-Blanc* that had been flung into the air by the explosion, plummeted to the ground. A section of the barrel of the large gun that had been positioned

Not even brick factories like this brewery in Dartmouth could withstand the force of the shock wave.
[Maritime Museum of the Atlantic]

on *Mont-Blanc*'s aft deck landed in Dartmouth, 3½ miles from the blast site. In Halifax, *Mont-Blanc*'s anchor shank—a chunk of metal that weighed 1,140 pounds—landed nearly 2½ miles away.

The explosion also created a tsunami—*tsunami* is a Japanese word that means "great harbor wave." A tsunami forms when a large quantity of ocean water rapidly shifts out of place. Most tsunamis are created when an earthquake occurs beneath the ocean floor. However, a very large explosion in a body of water can also trigger one. Within two minutes of the explosion, that's what happened in Halifax Harbour. The force of the blast instantly pushed the water away in all directions, creating a doughnut-shaped mound of water around the explosion site. In places where the water was very shallow, the bottom of the harbor was exposed. Upon reaching a certain height, the mound of water collapsed and spread out as a tsunami.

The crest of the tsunami was between 39 and 45 feet high. Along Richmond's waterfront, the wave's relentless push landward snapped the mooring lines of ships at their docks. It lifted the *Hilford*, a tugboat that was 64½ feet long, up and over the *Calonne* (one of the large ships that had been loading horses) and dropped it on top of Pier 9. It carried rowboats up onto shore, wedging them in the alleyways between ruined buildings. The wave swept people away as easily as if they were feathers. And then salt water quickly flowed across the land, much the same way it does after a wave crashes on a sandy beach. Survivors later recalled that there were puddles of salt water along Barrington Street, the road where the Pattison family lived.

At the same time it swamped Richmond's waterfront, the tsunami also spread outward, across the harbor, toward Dartmouth, Bedford Basin, and the mouth of the harbor. In less than two minutes, it crashed onto the Dartmouth shore, arriving as a wave as tall as 39 feet. It pushed *Imo* across the harbor and shoved her aground in Dartmouth. The combined force of the explosion and the tsunami carried the ship *Curaca*, which had been loading horses at Pier 8, over to Tufts Cove. On the shore near Tufts Cove, the tsunami quickly washed over and around the wreckage of homes in the Mi'kmaq settlement. George Dixon, a worker at a ship-building plant in Tufts Cove, later described the event: "When we got on our feet [after the blast] we looked around and saw a wave coming. . . . It went right up around the bungalows where we were working, right up on the land." Before the wave lost energy, water ran up as far as Windmill Road, the street where Gertrude Hook's family lived, a distance more than 700 feet inland.

In less than five minutes, an explosion—the likes of which the world had never seen before— and a tsunami had destroyed homes, factories, and businesses, wiping them from the land as though they had never existed. The effect on the people was far worse: Bodies and injured men, women, and children were everywhere.

The tsunami swept Imo *across the harbor, stranding her in the shallow water along the Dartmouth shore.* [Maritime Museum of the Atlantic]

⊰ 7 ⊱

THE END OF THE WORLD

A SHORT, TERRIBLE SILENCE followed the explosion. All the sounds of a lively city in 1917—wagon wheels rolling over cobblestones, horses neighing, railroad cars wheezing to a stop, the tram rumbling down its track, dogs barking, children laughing on their way to school, stevedores shouting out directions—simply stopped. Then, slowly, the survivors began to stir. And they found themselves surrounded by unimaginable horror. Smoke, water, and dead bodies. Blood everywhere, on everyone. In a flash, the shock wave and its effects killed more than a thousand people and left thousands more injured. The shock wave hurled people tens of feet from where they originally stood. Some were even tossed several city blocks away. Some survivors who had been at the bottom of the Fort Needham hill when the explosion occurred found themselves on top of the hill when they regained consciousness afterward. Hundreds of people lay buried in the ruins of their homes. As George Young, a Dartmouth schoolboy at the time of the explosion, later said,

"I thought it was the end of the world." As people struggled to make sense of the devastation, many of them reached the same conclusion: The Germans had attacked the city. They had bombed Halifax. That belief spread almost as fast as the fires that were already sweeping through the ruins of Richmond.

Piers 7, 8, and 9 were severely damaged; Pier 6 was completely gone. The tugboat *Stella Maris*, whose captain, Horatio Brannen, had led the efforts to extinguish the fire on *Mont-Blanc*'s deck, was badly damaged. Captain Brannen and eighteen members of his crew were dead; his son Walter and four other men were the only survivors. Four of the rescue crew from *Highflyer* and all six men in the small boat from *Niobe* were killed.

Mont-Blanc no longer existed; she had been completely obliterated. *Imo*, although damaged, was more or less still in one piece. The tsunami had beached her in Dartmouth. Her stunned crew was leaderless. Both Captain From and Pilot Hayes died during the explosion. Their bodies were later recovered in Dartmouth. Including the captain, six of *Imo*'s crew of thirty-nine men were dead.

RICHMOND IN RUINS

In Halifax, hundreds of people died instantly from the heat of the blast and the force of the shock wave, which was powerful enough to crush a person's internal organs. Vincent Coleman, in the railway office close to Pier 6, was among them. His telegraph key was found near his body. Albert O'Brien had just stepped off a boat in the dry dock area. He and more than one hundred people who were also in the dry dock died instantly. Vincent Pattison lay dead, buried deep beneath the brick rubble that had been the walls of the Acadia Sugar Refinery. George Richardson, the Indian School teacher, had been watching the fire outside his Barrington Street lodgings. He, too, died instantly. The Patricia was overturned, and, except for Billy Wells, all the firemen who had been riding in the fire pumper were killed. Constant Upham, the storekeeper who had telephoned the fire department, was also dead.

For many of Richmond's houses, the remnants of stone foundations were the only sign that a building had stood on that spot.
[City of Toronto Archives, Fonds 1244, Item 2435]

Several blocks away, Frances Coleman lay motionless on the kitchen floor inside her house, its plaster walls collapsed and shredded around her. The blast had flung little Eileen across the kitchen, where she lay trapped and crying under the kitchen sink. Soot and blood spattered her blue dress. Juanita, hurt and bleeding, one ear torn halfway off, staggered to her feet. Blood ran down her neck, dripping onto her clothes. She could see her mother's body covered with wood and plaster. Stunned and in shock, Juanita clambered over the rubble and tried to free her mother.

A few blocks away, inside St. Joseph's Church, Gerald Coleman lay surrounded by splintered boards. When he looked up, he could see the sky. The tall roof, shaped like an upside-down V, was gone. The church's arched windows gaped glassless. Unseen by Gerald, his friend Leo—the other altar boy—was trapped beneath a large wooden beam. Gerald scrambled through a hole in the wall and ran for home.

On the other side of the block, at St. Joseph's School, prayers stopped when the roof and floors collapsed, one on top of another, trapping the nuns and the students. The school's first floor ended up in the basement. Eleanor Coleman heard one of the nuns say that the Germans had attacked Halifax. Frightened, she wanted to go home, where she would be safe with her mother and sisters. Around her, classmates struggled to free themselves from the rubble and get out of the building. Some scrambled toward the broken staircase; others climbed up the water pipes until they reached the street level, where they could jump out through the broken windows. Eleanor clambered over boards and out of the ruined school. She looked toward the church and scarcely recognized it. Like her school, it was destroyed. Trees, blown flat, lay around the wreckage. She didn't see her brother anywhere. Even more scared, Eleanor ran for home, as her brother had.

Finding her house wasn't easy. All of Eleanor's usual landmarks lay in ruins. Burning coals from countless stoves smoldered in the rubble. In many places, flames already licked at the boards and smoke twisted upward. At the site of what had been the Coleman home, Eleanor joined Juanita and Gerald in frantically pulling plaster and boards away from their mother, who still lay motionless. Finally, they freed Frances and could see that although she was unconscious she was alive. Together, they rescued baby Eileen from beneath the sink and pulled their mother out into the street, where she soon regained consciousness. But when Frances tried to move, an agonizing pain stabbed through her. Although she didn't know it then, one of the bones in her back was broken.

Billy Wells, who had been driving the Patricia when the explosion occurred, had regained consciousness to find himself naked, his clothing entirely ripped from his body by the blast. His right arm was hurt and bleeding. In his left hand, he was still holding a piece of the steering wheel. Before he had time to think, the rushing water of the tsunami lifted his body and carried him away. When the wave set him down, he had no idea where the Patricia was. All he knew was that he had to find a hospital, so he set off walking down Barrington Street.

Lying flat on the ground in the middle of Barrington Street, James Pattison opened his eyes. He was sopping wet, covered with black, greasy soot and mud. There were puddles all over the road. Electric wires from the tram line, disconnected from their poles and luckily not sparking, lay draped across his body. After shoving them aside, he pushed himself up to his knees. When he wiped his face, his hand became blood-covered from his nose. And his hand hurt, because a metal nail was stuck in it. James pulled it out. Then, when he tried to wipe the blood from his hand, he noticed that his jacket was missing. Odd, because he knew he'd been wearing

After the explosion, St. Joseph's Church became a stone skeleton. [City of Toronto Archives, Fonds 1244, Item 2446]

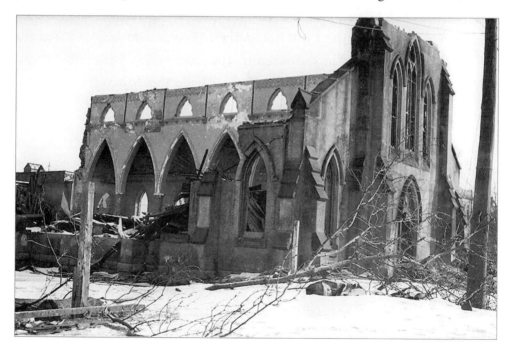

it when he left home. The leather backpack that he'd filled with books was gone too. He had no idea what had happened to either of them. James climbed over a jumble of stones alongside the road, which he gradually realized were the rocks that had formed a low wall around the orphanage a short distance from his house. The wall and the orphanage were gone.

In a daze, James looked around for his brothers, Gordon and Alan, but didn't see them. Another boy, however, covered with as much black soot as James was, stumbled unsteadily across the rubble. Like James, he had no jacket; one of his boots, the kind that laced up, was missing too. Then the boy raised his arm. That's when James saw it—the fancy screen that covered the face of Gordon's watch. The boy he hadn't recognized was his brother! Gordon and James looked for Alan, but they couldn't find him amid all the rubble. Still dazed and confused, the boys knew they had to go somewhere safe. Together, they started off down the street. The screams and cries of people who were injured or trapped in wreckage filled the air.

Unbeknownst to the boys, their mother, Annie, lay in the backyard of their home, in a space beneath a hodgepodge pile of boards. Just feet away, the boys' sister, Katharine, was trapped inside the tumbled-down ruins of the house. The house was already on fire.

Like everyone else, young Gerald O'Brien was covered with soot. He remembered that he had been on his way to the store. He'd been running down the street. But now he was lying on the ground in the alley between two houses. He had no idea how he had gotten there. People near him were running around, screaming and yelling. Gerald was confused and scared; he didn't know what else to do but go home. There, he found his family uninjured. His home, unlike many others, was still standing. But all the windows were gone, the plaster walls had cracked apart, and most of the furniture was broken. Later, when speaking of that day, his mother, Bertie, often said that after the explosion, her soup pot, which had been simmering on the stove, was filled with everything—glass, wood, and plaster—everything but soup. When Albert O'Brien did not return home, Bertie feared the worst. She couldn't leave her many young children unattended. She had no choice but to ask Evelyn, her eldest daughter, to try to find him.

Although the damage was less severe in neighborhoods farther from the blast site, destruction was widespread throughout Halifax. When the explosion occurred, ninth-grader Edith Doyle was in class at Chebucto School, about a mile inland from Pier 6, where *Mont-Blanc* ran aground. Because her teacher was late, the principal, Mr. Marshall, had stepped in and was giving the class a short science lesson. He had just asked the class for a definition of how sound travels when everyone felt a bump. Mr. Marshall explained that the bump was probably caused by a blast at the ocean terminal, where a new station was being built. He started to say that the sound of the explosion would follow—but his words were interrupted when a "terrific crash came and it just shook everything." Glass and plaster flew everywhere, and the classroom clock fell off the wall. Like others, Mr. Marshall thought the Germans had attacked. The students filed out of the school. When no further explosion occurred, Mr. Marshall sent Edith and the other students home.

Eleven-year-old Keith Allen lived two doors down from Chebucto School. He was late for school that morning and was still at home, coming down the stairs, when the blast occurred. He felt a gush of wind and suddenly found himself in the lower hallway. He had no idea how he had gotten there. The door of the house was splintered in half, none of the windows had glass in them, and crumbles of plaster from the walls surrounded him. Similar scenes could be found all over Halifax. And even though it lay across the harbor, Dartmouth suffered widespread damage too.

ACROSS HALIFAX HARBOUR

In the woods, not far from the Mi'kmaq settlement, Captain Le Médec and Pilot Mackey found themselves stunned, knocked down by the blast. Mackey's raincoat had been torn from his body as if it had been cut off at his waist. Fallen trees, with branches thicker than his arm, surrounded him. But neither he nor Le Médec was badly injured. The rest of *Mont-Blanc*'s crew survived the blast, too, though one crewman, who was severely injured by a piece of flying metal, died later. Eventually, Le Médec, Mackey, and the rest of the crew made their ways back to Halifax.

The Mi'kmaq settlement lay in shambles. The blast had

ripped through the Mi'kmaq community and torn apart the small homes. About two minutes later, the tsunami washed ashore, sweeping the wreckage along in a rush of water that caused additional destruction. Like many people in Halifax, Hannah Lonecloud and at least ten of her Mi'kmaq neighbors died instantly from the shock wave's force, which even at that distance was still strong enough to kill. Fallen timbers covered Rose MacDonald. Severely injured, she groaned in pain. Nearby, Murray was injured and burned from the hot blast. The MacDonald home was little more than a pile of splintered wood and tar paper. Mary, shoved against the stove by the blast, lay crying, her body badly burned. Harvey was unconscious. Flying debris had smashed into him

Like the Richmond and St. Joseph's schools in Halifax, the Indian School in Tufts Cove was completely destroyed. [Nova Scotia Archives and Records Management]

Before the explosion, the Cotton Factory had employed many workers. Little of the building remained afterward. [Maritime Museum of the Atlantic]

and shattered his arm bone. Another piece of debris was embedded in the back of his head. The side of his face was blistered with burns.

At the same time, on Windmill Road, Gertrude Hook was knocked to the floor. She was surprised to realize that she could see into the cellar. This was because another part of the floor had collapsed into the basement. In fact, the house had pretty much cracked down the middle and split apart. In the kitchen, her mother was calling for help. Gertrude hurried over and saw her mother struggling to lift the heavy iron stove, which had tipped over. Gertrude's brother Phillip lay on the floor, his leg pinned beneath the stove. Straining with all their might, Gertrude and her mother lifted the stove high enough for Phillip to pull his badly broken leg free. As she and her family left the house, Gertrude noticed that many of the nearby buildings, including the candy store across the way, were burning.

Throughout Richmond and Dartmouth, cries for help

and screams of pain filled the air. Injured people, thousands of them, were everywhere: walking or lying in the streets, crouched outside the wreckage of buildings, trapped aboard ships, buried inside collapsed buildings. Like James and Gordon Pattison, many of the survivors who had been outside found that their jackets, coats, and shoes were missing, blown off by the force of the shock wave. Others, who hadn't been wearing heavy garments, shivered in the cold, some naked, some left only with tatters. Mothers—often hurt and bleeding themselves—staggered in the streets, carrying their injured babies. Many of the survivors suffered broken bones.

Hundreds of people had been watching the fire through the windows of their homes and offices. Many bled from wounds to their bodies, faces, and eyes, caused when the panes shattered and knifelike glass shards hurled through the air. Julia Anne De Young, one of Eleanor Coleman's schoolmates at St. Joseph's, was running home. Like all the girls in the school, she wore a white apron over her dress. A policeman called out to her and asked for her apron. Julia gave it to him, then watched as he wrapped it around a man's bleeding eyes. Some people, like the man Julia saw, lost an eye; others were totally blinded. No matter what the nature of their injuries, it was clear that all of them needed help.

❖ 8 ❖

HELP!

WHEN THE EXPLOSION OCCURRED, telephone and telegraph communications instantly halted due to broken lines. For several hours, Halifax was isolated. Fortunately, Vincent Coleman's final telegraph message had set off an alarm that, like a row of dominoes falling, ran along the railway system from station to station. The message alerted the approaching train from Rockingham. Perhaps even more important, Mr. Coleman's heroic action notified other communities in Nova Scotia that something terrible had happened. Had he not telegraphed, it would have been many hours before anyone knew what had occurred. His timely message signaled that medical assistance would likely be needed. Doctors, nurses, and rescuers from all over Nova Scotia rushed to assemble supplies and make arrangements to travel to Halifax.

Even as Vincent Coleman's message was still being passed along, the people of Halifax and Dartmouth had begun rescue work. Men, women, and children hurried homeward in search of family members. Those who were able began digging through the rubble, many with their bare hands, moving whatever debris they could to rescue trapped and injured relatives. They tore sheets, tablecloths, and clothing into strips to bandage wounds. All around them, flames crackled. Seventeen-year-old Ethel Kidd, who lived near the southern edge of the Richmond neighborhood, joined friends who could do little more than watch as their houses burned. Afterward, she recalled, "There was no way of fighting the fire, because fire was everywhere you turned. Everything was on fire." Yet rescue efforts continued.

Within an hour of the explosion, the commanding

Fire engines steadily pumped water onto the fires, but putting them all out was an impossible task.
[Maritime Museum of the Atlantic]

officers in Wellington Barracks in Halifax and in other armed forces posts throughout the two-city area were busy issuing orders. They sent several hundred soldiers and sailors into the devastated neighborhoods on house-to-house search-and-rescue missions. Scores of people who might otherwise have died survived because so many soldiers were available at short notice. Immediately, police and firemen began round-the-clock duty. Similarly, off-duty doctors and nurses in Halifax and Dartmouth reported for service.

Top priority was given to transporting the injured to the hospitals in Halifax and Dartmouth, which were setting up additional ward space as best they could despite the damage to the buildings. Almost anything that could carry a person was used. Few people in the area owned cars, but those who did either volunteered their vehicle or found it commandeered

Ambulances made countless trips to the hospitals. Nurses like the woman in this picture worked around the clock providing care for the injured. [Maritime Museum of the Atlantic]

by soldiers. Soldier Ralph Procter, who was home in Halifax recovering from severe injuries he had received in France at the Battle of Vimy Ridge, drove people to hospitals all day long, even after the tires of his car had gone flat, punctured by broken glass, wire, and other sharp rubble. What he saw that day affected him more than anything he had experienced while serving in France. He later reported, "Over there you don't see women and children all broken to pieces." Ambulances and army trucks rushed to the scene. Many of the injured either climbed or were lifted onto large, flatbed wagons pulled by one or two horses or into smaller carts driven by soldiers. Still others were pushed to hospitals in wheelbarrows.

The train from Rockingham that Vincent Coleman tried to warn had halted a couple of miles outside the city; its cars swayed and its windows were shattered when the blast occurred. Seeing the smoke and hearing of the devastation, Mr. Gillespie, the conductor, instructed rescuers to begin loading injured and homeless people onto the train. When it was full, he took the train back along the same track to Truro, a town about 60 miles from Halifax, where the people could receive care.

In the confusion of transporting the injured to hospitals, family members were often separated from one another. Keeping track of who went where was almost impossible. Unconscious or severely injured adults couldn't identify themselves. Neither could babies too young to talk. Parents frantically searched for missing children from

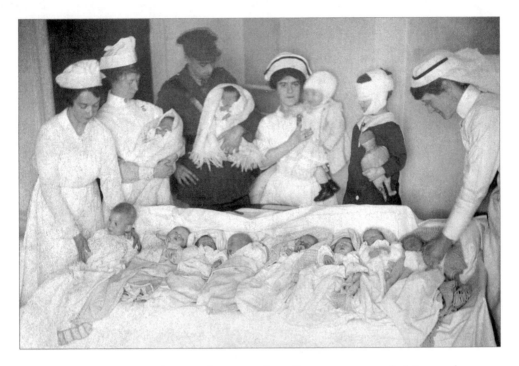

Many babies were separated from their families. Nurses cared for them while the authorities tried to reunite them with their parents.
[Maritime Museum of the Atlantic]

one hospital to another. In some cases, babies and young children were taken by train to other towns for treatment, making a relative's search almost hopeless.

The Coleman children and their mother, Frances, slowly made their way up Russell Street to Gottingen Street. Everywhere they looked, they saw flames and dismembered bodies. As they paused, wondering what to do, soldiers with a wagon pulled up alongside them. The family was transported to Camp Hill Military Hospital, where Frances was placed under a doctor's care and Juanita's ear was treated. At first, Eileen, the toddler, didn't appear badly hurt. But when a nurse laid the child back against a pillow to examine her, she realized the little girl had a large cut across the back of her head. She quickly reached for antiseptic and bandages.

Because she was severely injured, Frances had to remain in the hospital. Juanita and the other children were released after being treated. As the eldest, Juanita felt responsible for keeping her sisters and brother safe. But where should they go? Home was not an option—the house was gone, as were those of her neighbors. It was about 10:00 A.M., and she noticed people running uphill toward the Commons, a large open area where people normally played baseball and other games. Frightened that another bad thing was about to occur, Juanita decided that they would walk to their grandmother's house at the southern end of the city. Hopefully, they would be safe with her.

Around the same time, James and Gordon Pattison, after winding their way through the devastated Richmond streets, had stopped to rest on the Commons. There, people were sharing any extra warm clothing that they had with others who needed it. Suddenly more people began hurrying onto the Commons. As they rushed past James and Gordon, they shouted that the ammunition building at Wellington Barracks was on fire and likely to explode at any moment. To escape this new horror, people tried to get as far away from the Barracks as they could. Many fled to the Commons or to the Citadel, an old stone fort on the top of a large hill that overlooks Halifax Harbour. The report, however, was only a rumor. While there had been some small fires in Wellington Barracks, the soldiers had quickly extinguished them. In truth, the magazine had not been in danger of exploding. Sadly, the pandemonium that followed the rumor disrupted

Racing against time, sailors and soldiers searched the ruins for survivors. [City of Toronto Archives, Fonds 1244, Item 2449]

many rescue missions, wasting time badly needed to save more lives.

As others left the Commons, James and Gordon turned back in the direction of the waterfront. Soldiers prevented them from heading toward their home. Instead, the boys decided to find a boat that would take them across the harbor to Woodside, south of Dartmouth. Like the Coleman children, the Pattison boys chose to go to their grandparents' house for safety.

HOSPITALS EVERYWHERE
Recognizing how many people needed rapid assistance, Halifax city officials knew they had to work out a system to

supply aid in an organized way. In the city hall, shortly before noon, former mayor Robert MacIlreith was appointed to chair a meeting that quickly established committees to oversee transportation, delegate medical personnel, provide temporary hospitals and housing in various areas of the city, and distribute supplies and food. While many homes had been well stocked with food before the explosion—Annie Pattison later reported that her pantry had been full—after the explosion everything was covered with glass slivers, making the food inedible.

After the meeting concluded, MacIlreith set out on a sad task: locating a building to be used as a morgue, a place where the remains of the hundreds who had died could be kept until they were identified and claimed by relatives or friends. He chose Chebucto School, the same large, brick school where, only a few hours earlier, Edith Doyle had listened to her principal talk about sound.

In December 1917, Halifax and Dartmouth had four public hospitals, four military hospitals, and about seven small, private medical facilities. The combined total of all the available beds fell thousands short of the number needed. Docked at the Halifax yard for repairs, the USS *Old Colony* was a steamship from the United States that was soon to be retrofitted as a troop ship. She was quickly prepared as a temporary hospital, and injured people were taken aboard. Medical officers and doctors on emergency loan from other ships cared for the wounded.

Temporary hospital facilities and first aid stations sprang

Nurses sewed and prepared hundreds of bandages for the injured people.
[City of Toronto Archives, Fonds 1244, Item 2439]

up all over town, with cots set up in college halls, the Young Men's Christian Association (YMCA) building, an old prison, the theater in a music academy, the School for the Blind, church halls, and even in large private homes. People were carried into the hospitals by the hundreds. One of them was Gerald Coleman's friend Leo, who had been pulled from the wreckage of St. Joseph's Church and taken to the Nova Scotia Hospital. He later died from his injuries. As people became aware of the magnitude of the disaster—more than six thousand were injured and approximately nine thousand were left homeless— many residents whose houses had not been seriously damaged offered rooms to refugees who needed a place to recover.

By afternoon, doctors, nurses, and rescue workers from other towns in Nova Scotia arrived in Halifax to bring supplies and help the overwhelmed medical workers. Dr. Willis Moore arrived from Kentville, Nova Scotia, on one of the first relief trains into Halifax. He was sent to Camp Hill Military Hospital, where he immediately began treating patients. The sheer number of them astounded him. He later wrote, "Men, women, and children of all sorts and classes were literally packed in the wards like sardines in a box, the cots all occupied, and the floors covered so that it was often difficult to step between them." The terrible injuries were almost more than he, even as a trained doctor, could bear to see. He also wrote that many of the patients were in a stunned state, moving and responding but seemingly not aware of what was happening. "So numbed by shock were they, that many did not appear to need an anesthetic [or pain killer] for treatments that normally would require them." Moore also "marveled greatly" at the medical relief that the doctors and nurses of Halifax had been able to accomplish under the most difficult of circumstances with little help.

Sometime that day, a sailor from the USS *Old Colony* rescued Annie Pattison from the debris in her backyard. He brought her to the YMCA building, where a doctor treated her burns, bruises, and badly broken right hand. By then, James and Gordon had arrived at their grandparents' house. They did not yet know that their mother had been rescued. Nor did they know what had happened to Katharine, Alan, or their father.

Meanwhile, in Dartmouth, Gertrude Hook's brother Phillip was unable to walk on his broken leg. Soldiers carried him in a wheelbarrow to a large house that had been set up as a temporary hospital. Having been turned away from the house where Phillip was being treated, Gertrude and her mother, who was pushing the two youngest children in a carriage, headed toward Albro Lake, a wooded area where many of their neighbors had gone. Because the lake was more than a mile from the harbor, it seemed that it would be a safe place to stay in case there was another explosion.

In Tufts Cove, Rose MacDonald lay helpless, pinned by timber as rescuers sought to help her. Severely injured and in pain, Rose asked someone to please send a priest to her. Rose died before he could arrive. Harvey was taken, unconscious, to one of the temporary hospitals, as were Murray and Mary.

MORE HELP

Relief trains from other areas of Nova Scotia continued to arrive. As soon as he heard about the explosion, Jerry Lonecloud, who was in Kentville, Nova Scotia, about 60 miles from Halifax, boarded a relief train, determined to get home to his daughters and grandchildren. When the train stopped about nine miles from Tufts Cove, Lonecloud left it and walked the rest of the way. Arriving in Dartmouth that evening, he heard the terrible news that Hannah and Rose were dead. He clung to the hope that his grandchildren still lived.

Even as other Nova Scotians made their way to Halifax, word of the disaster spread throughout Canada and into the

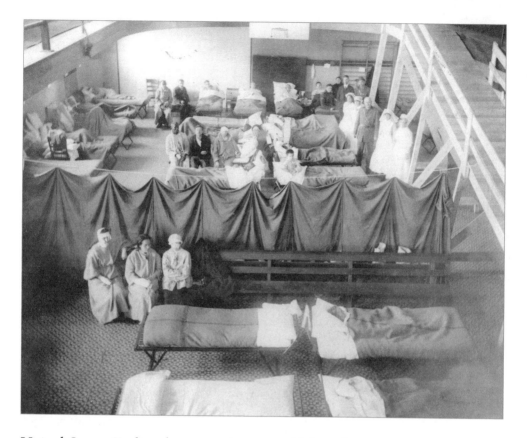

Temporary hospitals like this one at the YMCA on Barrington Street were set up in various places throughout Halifax and Dartmouth.
[Nova Scotia Archives and Records Management]

United States. Earlier that year, the state of Massachusetts had established the Massachusetts Committee on Public Safety. Because the United States was at war, people worried about what would happen if the country were attacked. The committee was essentially an emergency response team. To create a knowledgeable base, members of the committee came from various professions, such as medical care, transportation, food, housing, and communications. It also included government officials. Together, they had discussed what kinds of disasters might occur and the best ways to respond to those emergency situations in terms of their respective fields.

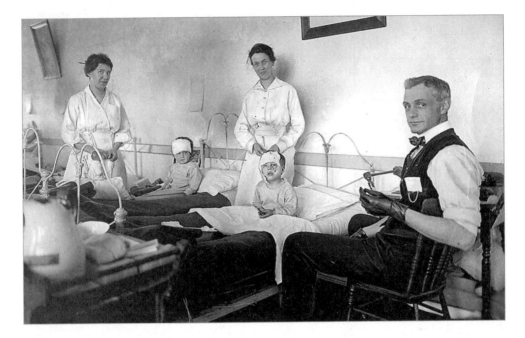

Many of the beds in hospital wards were occupied by injured children. [City of Toronto Archives, Fonds 1244, Item 1782]

By noon on December 6, Massachusetts governor Samuel McCall had heard about the Halifax disaster and called together members of the committee. Although information was sketchy, it was clear that a lot of doctors, nurses, and supplies—medical and for building or repairing homes— were desperately needed. Wasting no time, the committee made arrangements for a relief train to go to Halifax. Governor McCall placed Abraham C. Ratshesky in charge as the commissioner of the Halifax Relief Expedition. He gave Ratshesky a letter of introduction to the mayor of Halifax, which read, in part,

> I am sending Hon[orable] A. C. Ratshesky of the Massachusetts Public Safety Committee, immediately to your city, with a corps of our best State surgeons and nurses, in the belief that they may be of service to you in the hour of need. . . . We have

the strongest affection for the people of your city, and . . . we are anxious to do everything possible for their assistance at this time. . . . Assure them that we are ready to answer any call that they may need to make upon us.

By 10:00 P.M. the train, stocked with bandages, medicines, surgical equipment, twelve surgeons, ten nurses, representatives from the American Red Cross, and several newspaper reporters, rolled out of Boston.

In Halifax, by nine o'clock that night, army personnel had erected a tent city that covered a large area of the Commons. Some of the tents served as first aid stations. Containing food and blankets—some even had a small stove—they provided shelter for a few hundred of the homeless. Unfortunately, many of the tents went unoccupied. After seeing sturdy homes so easily destroyed, some people feared the tents could provide little or no safety.

Before going to bed, Keith Allen helped his father nail boards across the windows in their house. Nearly twelve, he had been a big help to his mother earlier in the day, shoveling the broken glass on the floors into a coal scuttle and dumping it outside. But when it was time for bed, Keith trembled with fear and shook at every loud noise. It wasn't until he climbed into his father's bed and snuggled close beside him that he felt safe enough to fall asleep.

Throughout the night, rescuers and family members, oil lanterns in hand, continued their search for survivors. Flames from the burning buildings flickered in the darkness, but their heat provided little comfort to the searchers. The terrible truth was that even as those flames warmed the rescuers, they spelled certain death for the many people who lay trapped inside the burning ruins. Every minute, their hopes for rescue grew dimmer. All night long, cries for help filled the air. And yet another force—as if explosion, injury, tsunami, and flames weren't enough—began brewing, one that would slam Halifax and Dartmouth the next day.

As night approached, the Commons became a city of tents set up to provide shelter for the homeless.
[Maritime Museum of the Atlantic]

A TURN FOR THE WORSE

IN THE EARLY MORNING of Friday, December 7, rescue efforts continued under threatening gray skies. A cold, northeast breeze blew across the region. By 9:00 A.M. snow was falling. The roads were already wet from the tsunami, the black rain, and the fire hoses; now they became even slicker. Throughout the morning, the intensity of the wind increased and it snowed harder. By afternoon, a full-force blizzard pummeled the area. Driving snow blinded the rescuers and hampered relief efforts. Cars and trucks became useless, their wheels mired in the deepening snow.

During the blizzard after the explosion, Arthur Lismer, a famous Canadian artist, sketched the horses and sleds as they carried bodies to the mortuary. [Arthur Lismer, 1917 (licensor Janet Cauffiel)]

Horses strained against their harnesses, scrambling to keep from falling as they trudged through the heavy snowdrifts that quickly formed

around the ruins. Women in long dresses and overcoats floundered in the snow, falling and picking themselves up again and again as they searched for missing loved ones. Rescuers still traveling to Halifax found their journeys halted. Even the relief train from Boston was temporarily delayed by the snowdrifts that covered the railroad tracks.

In buildings everywhere, including the hospitals, people tried to block the relentless wind and driving snow by nailing boards, blankets, and carpeting across broken windows. All through the day, doctors and nurses and volunteers from Halifax and Dartmouth cared for the injured. Without rest, they stitched wounds, set broken bones, examined eyes—and in many cases removed them. It was soon apparent that caring for the injured would take more than a few days.

Despite the blizzard, the grim task of collecting bodies from the streets and the ruins continued. Large flatbed wagons, drawn by teams of horses, creaked and trundled up and down the streets, collecting the remains of the dead, many burned beyond recognition. Blankets draped the heavy loads, but everyone knew what lay beneath—and prayed that the wagons didn't carry a member of their family.

Preparations for receiving the dead at Chebucto School were finished. The basement was swept free of broken glass. Tar paper and boards covered the windows, protecting the workers inside from the weather. It also preserved the dignity of the dead and created some privacy for family members as they looked for their loved ones. Materials to embalm, or preserve, some of the remains were ready for use. There were too many bodies to preserve all of them, but the remains of children were to be embalmed in the hope that a few extra days in the morgue would allow a parent more time to find his or her child. From the steps of his house, young Keith Allen watched "as the wagons . . . came with bodies piled on them . . . many of them little children." Trip after trip, the wagons rolled down Keith's street, carrying remains to his school.

Through a tragic quirk of fate, the people of Halifax had experience with operating a morgue that contained a large number of unidentified bodies. Five and a half years earlier, in April 1912, the ocean liner *Titanic* had sunk after hitting an iceberg. More than 1,500 people had

To prevent any unauthorized people from entering the devastated area, the authorities issued passes; those without them were not permitted to go in.
[Nova Scotia Archives and Records Management]

City of Halifax   No. 15264

Pass for Devastated Area

Allow Bearer within Devastated District

NAME _____

FRANK HANRAHAN
Chief of Police

drowned. Most of the bodies were not recovered. Two hundred nine bodies that were found shortly after the accident were sent to Halifax, the closest city to the disaster site with shipping and railway facilities that could transport the remains to places where they could be claimed for burial. All the bodies received in Halifax had had to be identified or described in some way. John Barnstead, the coroner for the city of Halifax, developed a numbering system to do so, and this was used again for the victims of the harbor explosion in 1917.

Every set of remains and any personal effects found with them, or even nearby, such as jewelry, hair combs, watches, papers, or wallets, were labeled as they were collected, including the street address or the location where the body was found. If a name was known, it was included on the label. In addition, a description of the individual was jotted down at the morgue. For example, one label read "Male, approx 38.

On the morning of December 6, before he left home for school, a boy named James Fraser shoved these items into his pocket. They were found with his body.
[Maritime Museum of the Atlantic]

Dark hair, med dark complexion, good teeth. Blue overalls. Blue sailor's sweater. . . . Brass cufflinks. Black pants. One black handled 2 bladed knife. Gold signet ring on 3rd finger of right hand with monogram SS."

To prevent one person's possessions from getting mixed with those of another, each set of remains and the associated possessions received the same number. The possessions were placed in a labeled cloth bag that closed with a drawstring. Collecting the effects led to some accusations that soldiers were stealing from the dead, no doubt fueled by reports that soldiers had been seen cutting rings to remove them from fingers. In fact, they had reason to do so: Because a body swells as it begins to decompose after death, the only way soldiers could remove some of the rings was by cutting them off. Rings, like other items that might be identified by family members, were removed before burial with the hope that they might be recognized at some future time by a friend or relative, thereby giving a name to another of the nameless dead. (Many unclaimed possessions, including cut rings, later became part of the explosion collection in the Maritime Museum of the Atlantic.)

Within twenty-four hours, remains draped with sheets filled the basement of Chebucto School, lying on low wooden platforms that lined the floor. Soldiers, policemen, and volunteers accompanied people as they sought missing relatives. Daily, the newspapers published long lists of people who had died; families put notices in the papers that listed relatives who were missing. And for days, despite a second blizzard

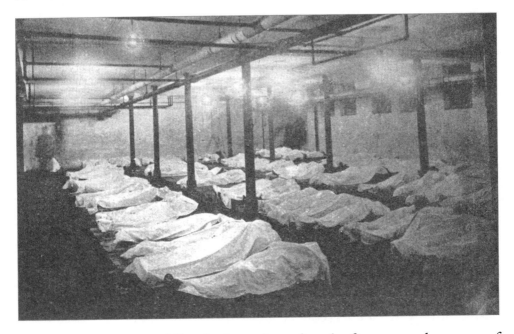

There were so many bodies that Chebucto School had to be used as a mortuary. People went there to find their missing loved ones. [Nova Scotia Archives and Records Management]

that fell only three days after the first, a steady stream of family members continued to walk through the morgue.

In their grandparents' home, James and Gordon Pattison received hopeful information from their uncles, who had been searching the Halifax hospitals for the boys' mother, Annie. She was alive and being cared for in the YMCA hospital. Shortly afterward, however, one uncle returned home with heart-wrenching news. He had identified their brother Alan's body in the morgue. And the remains of the boys' sister, Katharine, had been found amid the blackened ruins of their house on Barrington Street. Their father, Vincent Pattison, was still missing.

Evelyn O'Brien trudged throughout the city, from hospital to hospital, looking for her father. She dreaded going to the morgue, but after searching for three days, she had no alternative. After walking up and down the rows, she suddenly stopped at one draped body. Even without lifting the sheet, she knew who it was: Albert O'Brien had had a problem with his feet that required him to wear specially made shoes. Evelyn recognized his shoes, which had been left uncovered.

Frances Coleman, in pain in her hospital bed, was devastated to learn that her husband's remains had been identified at the morgue. Mr. Coleman's body was so severely burned that his brother identified it only by recognizing his watch and wallet, which accompanied his body.

In Dartmouth, Harvey MacDonald briefly regained consciousness and found he was in a building that seemed like a school to him. He was confused because he was lying in a bed, like at a hospital. The back of his head hurt. His arm and his feet hurt. But before he could think about the pain very much, he lost consciousness again. He faded in and out of awareness for a long time. Once when he was awake, he noticed that patches of his skin were imbedded with black soot. Another time, Harvey heard his father's voice. When

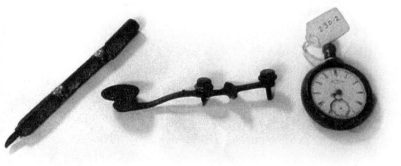

Vincent Coleman's telegraph key and pen were found in the ruins of the railway station. His watch was found with his body.
[Maritime Museum of the Atlantic]

he opened his eyes, he saw that his father had passed right by his bed without recognizing him. Harvey cried out until his father heard him and turned back. At some point, someone—Harvey couldn't remember who—told him that his mother, Rose; his brother, Murray; and his sister, Mary, had all died.

Meanwhile, Gertrude Hook and her family had reunited. Her father had returned unharmed from his job in Halifax, and her two older sisters—who had been moved to safety with other students—had rejoined them in a church hall, where they stayed overnight. Her brother Phillip was being cared for in a hospital. Blankets covered the church's broken windows, and it was dark inside, but Gertrude didn't care. Her family was alive. The next day they moved into a friend's house, where they stayed until they could make arrangements for the future.

All over Halifax and Dartmouth, families searched lists posted in hospitals and first aid stations for news of their loved ones. As information trickled in, some of it led to joyous reunions; some did not. Meanwhile, those without homes scrambled to find shelter in the homes of friends or in other buildings, such as schools and churches.

MEDICAL HELP FROM OUTSIDE

During the first twenty-four hours after the explosion, the doctors, nurses, and citizens of Halifax, plus those from other towns in Nova Scotia who arrived in the city before the first blizzard struck, stretched themselves to their

American relief workers stand outside one of the temporary hospitals.
[Nova Scotia Archives and Records Management]

limits and then pushed themselves beyond exhaustion. Countless lives were saved as the result of their dedication. But caring for the injured was a huge job and required many more doctors and nurses. By December 7, newspapers such as the *Daily Echo* began carrying notices—some as large as a quarter of the news page—that read "If You Want Accommodation, or if You Will Supply Accommodation for Homeless and for Nurses and Doctors, Notify Immediately the Registrar's Office at the City Hall." The doctors gratefully welcomed the arrival of trains loaded with medical personnel and supplies from other provinces and the United States.

The Halifax Relief Expedition train from Boston, which had collected more supplies and more relief workers at almost every stop along its way to Halifax, didn't arrive as quickly as

Sledding after the blizzard was serious business. These children are using sleds to haul much-needed supplies from a relief station to their families. [Nova Scotia Archives and Records Management]

hoped. When the train reached St. John, the capital of New Brunswick, the province northwest of Nova Scotia, the blizzard's heavy snow had reduced visibility to nearly zero. "An enormous snowdrift [that] lay across the track" finally halted the train. Commissioner Ratshesky begged the railroad officials to help them, explaining the importance of the train and its cargo to the suffering people in Halifax. According to Ratshesky, a group of men sympathetic to the expedition's cause shoveled the huge drift away and "amid great cheers from all on board, we went through the drift, which extended higher than the door of the baggage car." The train rolled into Halifax at 3:00 A.M. on Saturday, December 8. It was the first relief train to arrive from the United States.

The members of the relief expedition immediately made their way to city hall. At one point in their journey downtown, they were driven in a vehicle that had already seen heavy use transporting injured people to hospitals and the dead to the morgue. Ratshesky later wrote, "The young man driver had lost all the members of his family, consisting of his wife and four children." The relief team was instructed to set up a temporary hospital in the large downtown Bellevue Building. Although it had been damaged by the explosion, they busily cleaned up the glass, water, and ice-covered floors with the help of sailors from the USS *Old Colony*. Within several hours, the people from Massachusetts were moving in furniture and setting up operating facilities to accommodate patients.

During wartime, distressing news is a regular occurrence. Lists of war dead and wounded were regularly published in newspapers. But the Halifax disaster, so much closer to home than the war in Europe, touched a special chord in everyone who heard about it. Offers of help and supplies poured in. The state of Maine sent five train cars filled with supplies and ten thousand wool blankets. The Massachusetts Automobile Club sent ten trucks. Schoolchildren in St. John, New Brunswick, donated ten thousand pieces of children's clothing. A Red Cross train from New York carried mattresses, blankets, food, and clothes.

Mrs. James Slayter, whose family lived in Halifax, volunteered to sort clothing sent from the United States by its size and type so the garments could be distributed to the appropriate people. She was especially touched by one shipment: A surprise of some sort—perfume, a box of talcum powder, a small toy—had been placed in the pocket of every outfit. And all the garments were clean and in excellent condition.

Melting snow soaked some of the clothing sent in the relief boxes. Before the clothes could be sorted at the distribution center, they were dried at Ungar's Laundry—the place where Evelyn O'Brien worked. According to Mrs. Slayter, "Women working at the relief were so cold that when a lot of freshly dried clothes would come over from the laundry, they would all run to put their hands among them because they were [still] warm from the drying-room."

Many people donated money. So did local and national governments, some giving millions of dollars. In addition to the relief trains from Boston, the citizens of Massachusetts later donated $700,000 U.S. dollars to the Massachusetts-Halifax Relief Fund. Most of the money was used to purchase a wide variety of furniture that was placed in a large warehouse. People who needed tables, dressers, chairs, beds,

Standing in the middle of Barrington Street and looking north, all a person could see was devastation.
[Nova Scotia Archives and Records Management]

and other furniture could go there and choose what items best suited their needs.

It wasn't only people who were affected by the explosion. Many animals were lost, injured, or left homeless too. Keith Allen had a little brown dog named Jacky, who often followed his father to work at the North Street Railroad Station. Worried that Jacky would get run over by a train, Keith's father always locked the dog inside his office at the station. That's what he'd done on the morning of the explosion. Keith's family was relieved when Mr. Allen arrived home safely. But he told them that Jacky had been in the building when it collapsed. Keith believed he would never see his pet again. The next day, a little black dog trotted up to Keith's house. It was Jacky—totally covered with soot, but

The Massachusetts-Halifax Relief Committee's furniture warehouse distributed furniture to thousands of residents. [Nova Scotia Archives and Records Management]

alive and unhurt. Somehow he had dug his way out of the ruined station and run home, where he was happily reunited with Keith.

Many other animals weren't as lucky. Injured horses and cows had to be humanely destroyed. Other animals, such as hens and pigs, no longer had a coop or barn to live in. They simply roosted in the rubble or roamed the streets. Again, the people of Massachusetts stepped in: The Society for the Prevention of Cruelty to Animals sent a thousand U.S. dollars to buy food and find homes for homeless animals. As relief of all kinds poured in, the initial shock of the disaster lessened, and grief and anger took its place. People wanted to know who was to blame for their losses.

The explosion left many animals homeless. At first, they had to fend for themselves and take shelter wherever they could find it.
[City of Toronto Archives, Fonds 1244, Item 2443]

Five of Mont-Blanc's *crewmen. Only one crewmember died as a result of the explosion.* [Maritime Museum of the Atlantic]

A number of the testimonies were contradictory, and the attorney representing *Imo*'s interests often used bullying tactics when he questioned witnesses who spoke on behalf of *Mont-Blanc*. Despite reports that the harbor's rules of safe travel had not been followed and repeated mention of the confusing exchange of signals between *Imo* and *Mont-Blanc* (and possibly other ships in the harbor), Judge Drysdale ruled that Captain Le Médec and Pilot Francis Mackey were solely responsible for the collision. The judge recommended that Le Médec lose his captaincy and that Mackey's license be revoked and he be prosecuted in criminal court. Mackey spent a short time in jail, but he was released after another trial was held. Eventually, he resumed his job piloting ships in Halifax Harbour and Captain Le Médec returned to France. *Imo* was repaired and renamed *Guvernoren*. She was used as a whale oil tanker until she ran onto the rocks off the coast of South America and was abandoned in 1921.

Even after *Imo* began her other life, the quest to determine who was to blame for the collision continued as attorneys for the owners of *Mont-Blanc* appealed the case twice in higher courts. The last of these appeals, held in February 1920, took place in the Privy Council in London, England. This was the court of last resort. And the decision of the justices in this court was that both captains were equally at fault.

FINAL GOOD-BYES

For a week after the explosion, a steady stream of people came to the Chebucto School morgue. When a family member positively identified a body, he or she was given a burial permit, and the remains were released for private burial. Funeral services for families and for the military occurred daily. However, some bodies had no one to claim them— some of the sailors, for example, had been from England, Norway, Finland, Jamaica, and China. In other cases, an entire family had been killed or relatives were too injured to come to the morgue. These remains lay unclaimed, as did those too badly burned to be identified. As the days passed, despite additional bodies still being removed daily from the wreckage, it became necessary to bury the unidentified dead.

The afternoon of December 17, in the schoolyard alongside Chebucto School, members of the clergy conducted two burial services, one Protestant and one Catholic.

Several thousand people joined in as prayers were said over ninety-five unidentified bodies. Following the services, soldiers loaded the coffins onto trucks and wagons and carried them to their final resting places in Fairview and Mount Olivet cemeteries. In both cemeteries, the graves of the unidentified victims are grouped together in the same area.

In mid-January 1918, more than a month after the explosion, soldiers stopped searching for remains in the wreckage. Yet even as the area was cleared for recovery and rebuilding, victims continued to be discovered. For the Pattison family, the ordeal of not knowing Vincent's fate was prolonged: His remains, buried in the ruins of the sugar refinery, were not found until April 1918. The upsetting task of identifying

Vincent's body fell to his oldest son, Gordon. He could do so only because he recognized his brother James's pocket watch—the one Mr. Pattison had borrowed while his own was being repaired—with his father's remains. Although rusted by water during its five-month exposure to weather in the refinery ruins, the imprint of the two watch hands remained clear: ten minutes past nine—the time of the explosion plus the five extra minutes that Vincent Pattison had added to avoid being late to work.

Officially, the number of deaths directly attributed to the explosion is 1,952—nearly 500 of whom were children. In reality, most historians believe that more than 2,000 people died.

LOST AND ORPHANED

Within a week of the explosion, it quickly became clear that injured, lost, and orphaned children were a serious problem. The tally was daunting: Seventy children had been orphaned; more than two hundred were left with only one surviving parent. In some cases, that parent was too injured to care for the child. In other cases, the surviving parent was a father who was serving in the war in Europe. Halifax had several orphanages. Many of them needed repairs due to the explosion; one had been destroyed completely. A separate committee was formed and charged to repair damaged orphanages, make sure children in custody were being cared for properly, provide clothes for the children, and try to locate a parent or relative. If that wasn't possible, they tried to arrange an adoption.

Accomplishing these goals took time, according to each circumstance. Letters from caring people in other provinces and in the United States carried offers to adopt orphaned children. After Albert O'Brien's death, some people approached his widow, Bertie, and asked if they could adopt one of her ten children. Bertie was appalled and quickly told them no. But many orphaned children were adopted. The adoptions were monitored by the government, and children were not allowed to go to distant homes where they could not be supervised by the committee. Some went to good homes, but a few later said that they were treated like servants.

Every day, the newspapers carried descriptions of missing and unclaimed children. Happily, some of them were reunited with their families. Nine-year-old Edward Hartlen survived the explosion with a broken arm and his eyes badly wounded by glass. He was taken by train to a hospital in New Glasgow, a town about 100 miles from Halifax. Believed to have been orphaned, Edward remained in New Glasgow for almost eight months. He was on the verge of being adopted when a minister in town sent a letter about Edward to the committee in Halifax. It turned out Edward's family was still alive and had been searching for him.

Children with a single surviving parent who was unable to care for them due to injury, or because the parent was fighting in the war, stayed in an orphanage until they could

be claimed. Sadly, sometimes even children with an unin-jured surviving parent were put into orphanages. A situation like this could occur if the parent had to work all day and the child still needed medical care. Some of these children were eventually adopted by other families. That's what happened to Harvey MacDonald. For some months, he lived in an orphanage because his father—who had been living apart from the family at the time of the explosion—was unable to care for him. In fact, Harvey eventually lost all contact with his father, James MacDonald, and also with his grand-parents, Jerry and Elizabeth Lonecloud. Fortunately, a family whose last name was Murray took Harvey to live with them.

Pine coffins containing the bodies of explosion victims lined George and Argyle streets. Snow and Company, Undertakers, is the second building from the right.
[Nova Scotia Archives and Records Management]

They loved him and treated him as though he'd always been a member of their family. And although he missed his mother, brother, and sister, he loved the Murrays, too. Other children remained in orphanages until they were old enough to work and live on their own.

⊰ II ⊱

RECOVERY AND RECONSTRUCTION

IN THE DAYS AND WEEKS following the explosion, people began making efforts to resume their lives. Carpenters, stone-masons, glaziers (people who fix windows), bricklayers, and general laborers flooded the city as reconstruction efforts started. Some of the houses, though nearly in shambles, could still be lived in. As long as a family had a stove for providing heat, they moved back in. Often only one or two rooms in these houses were habitable. At times, that created awkward living conditions.

When the Fenerty family returned to their seven-room house, only one room still had walls. For days, the nine members of the family—who ranged in age from four to forty-nine years—shared that room. Maude Fenerty, who was twenty years old at the time of the explosion, later recalled that privacy was essentially nonexistent. At bath time, everyone but the person taking a bath would have to go outside. In the mornings, Maude's mother used to make the boys and girls get up separately. When the boys were out of the room, the girls got dressed. The boys dressed after the girls finished. They all lived this way until Maude's father and reconstruction laborers had time to build some creative temporary walls. They ripped sheets of linoleum from the floors and nailed them onto a wooden framework. The result looked like patchwork, but the Fenertys didn't mind. Before the explosion there had been ten members of the family. During the explosion, sixteen-year-old George Fenerty had been killed at the railroad yard. For the grieving family, being together at such a sad time was far more important than worrying about tight living quarters.

The relief committees established immediately after the blast did an admirable job getting emergency medical care, temporary shelter, and supplies such as food and blankets to the survivors. Within days, soldiers began building

This photo, looking north in the area around Duffus Street, was taken in June 1918. Most of the ruins had been cleared away so reconstruction could begin. [Nova Scotia Archives and Records Management]

temporary apartments on the Commons. These apartments, with two, three, or four rooms, provided housing for about a thousand people. By March 1918, forty more buildings, each containing eight apartments, had been erected on a large open area called the Exhibition Grounds. Named the Governor McCall Apartments, in honor of Massachusetts governor Samuel McCall, the two-story buildings housed more than two thousand people. From the outside, the tar-paper-covered buildings were not fancy to look at. But each apartment rented for as much as twelve dollars per month, had four rooms, and came equipped with a stove, water heater, bathroom, sink, and running water. Compared with living in a tent or in one room, the McCall Apartments seemed quite comfortable. Similar apartments were also built in Dartmouth, but not as many.

Temporary Houses

ALL persons rendered homeless by the disaster who will require accommodation in the new houses now being erected, and who have not already applied for one are requested to make immediate application by mail.

The following are the types of houses at present being built:—

                            per month.

Class "A"—4 rooms and bath: rent $12.00

Class "B"—4 rooms and bath, slightly smaller rooms than Class "A": rent $10.00

Class "C"—3 rooms, no bath: rent ....$ 7·50

Class "D"—2 rooms, no bath: rent ....$ 5.00

Class "A" houses are at the Exhibition Grounds.

Class "A" and "B" houses on the South Common.

Class "C" and "D" houses on the Citadel Football Grounds.

Kindly fill out the application below and mail it at once.

APPLICATION

Name ....

Former address ....

Number of adults in family ....

Number of children in family ....

Which type of house do you want? ....

At which place do you wish to live? ....

Address to:

J. H. WINFIELD,

Chairman, Rehabilitation Committee, St. Mary's Army and Navy Club, Barrington Street, City.

7269 h 15 m dy 19.

While the temporary relief committees did outstanding work, it was necessary to develop and manage long-term plans for providing shelter and services to the survivors. On January 21, 1918, a permanent Halifax Relief Commission officially took over these matters. The commission had the authority to dispense, as it saw fit, the monies that had been donated by other provinces in Canada, other governments

People filled out applications like this one to receive assignments of temporary housing.
[Nova Scotia Archives and Records Management]

Construction workers sawed and hammered together thousands of feet of lumber as they built the McCall Apartments.
[City of Toronto Archives, Fonds 1244, Item 2447]

throughout the world, and the general public. This amounted to nearly $21 million. Reconstruction was one of the commission's duties. It hired laborers to repair damaged homes and build new ones; home owners could also apply to the commission for money to repair their dwellings.

THE HYDROSTONE

A plan for the permanent reconstruction of the Richmond area was necessary. The Halifax Relief Commission began an ambitious building project toward that goal. It reclaimed land from property owners on the western side of Fort Needham. Then, eighty-eight buildings—a mix of duplex and single-family homes for 324 families—were built along a newly laid out grid of boulevards. Each boulevard featured a

The children in this picture lived in the McCall Apartments. The baby in the carriage is Charles Vaughan, who grew up to become a mayor of Halifax. The man second from the left is Massachusetts governor Samuel W. McCall, for whom the apartments are named.

[Maritime Museum of the Atlantic]

CONSTRUCTION   57

HYDRO-STONE

The Material Used in Rebuilding Halifax

as specified by Ross & Macdonald, Architects.

HYDRO-STONE was used in the erection of over 300 houses of permanent construction, and no other material would have answered the requirements so well as HYDRO-STONE.

The views reproduced show a block of HYDRO-STONE just delivered from the machine and blocks being loaded on cars for shipment from the yards at Halifax to the building lots.

HYDRO-STONE is a building unit made of properly proportioned aggregate, consisting of gravel or crushed stone, sand and Portland cement, with sufficient water to crystallize it thoroughly. In the making, each unit is subjected to 150,000 pounds pressure, resulting in a unit that has a smaller percentage of absorption than any other building material. This pressure forces the excess moisture to the surface at all points and compacts the aggregates so closely that a perfect bond is insured, giving maximum density and strength.

HYDRO-STONE is hardened in wet live steam, which causes all the moisture to be retained until thorough crystallization has taken place. This results in a hard dense concrete unit with sharp, clean edges.

Made in any size, shape or design desired. Any color scheme can be followed with excellent results. You should investigate this new and important building material. Send for particulars.

HYDRO-STONE COMPANY

Second Floor   Insurance Building
Chicago, Illinois

A Block for Every Wall
A Wall for Every Purpose

Hydro-Stone was a building material made of crushed stone, cement, and sand. [Nova Scotia Archives and Records Management]

grass-covered parkway that ran the length of the street, on which trees would be planted. The development's planner hoped to create a neighborhood with plenty of open space, similar to an English garden town. (The garden town concept includes a lot of communal park space, as well as a yard for every home.) Six different house plans created diversity and appeal, and a group of shops built along one end of the development would bring commerce to the new neighborhood. But there was an aspect of the development that many people did not like: All the buildings were owned by the Halifax Relief Commission, to which the residents paid a monthly rent. Even if a family had owned a home in the area previously, renting was the only option available in the new development. (In 1949, the commission began letting residents buy the homes.)

Builders constructed the homes and stores with blocks produced in a town south of Dartmouth and made of a material called Hydro-Stone, a composite of crushed stone, sand,

and Portland cement. Using Hydro-Stone as the building material had specific appeal for the city: Unlike wood, it is fire resistant. Barges carried the blocks across the harbor, where they were loaded onto railway cars and delivered to the site on a specially built train track. By the end of March 1919, families had moved into the first completed homes.

During the next two years, more houses were added, as were shops such as a grocery, a shoe store, a bank, and a pharmacy. Construction of the neighborhood, which came to be called the Hydrostone, was completed in 1921. Although two thousand people lived in the neighborhood, there weren't enough dwellings for everyone who wanted one. Some people were bitter that they had not been provided with a home

The Hydrostone houses, providing comfortable living quarters and attractive outdoor green space, were much sought after by those who had lost their homes. Today, the Hydrostone area is a trendy neighborhood.
[Sally M. Walker]

there and, like others who had not received aid, felt their families had been abandoned.

The Hydrostone, however, was only one neighborhood being reconstructed. After clearing the land between Fort Needham and the harbor, which had been more severely damaged than the Hydrostone area, people began rebuilding. Some of the new homes were built with Hydro-Stone; many were built of wood. Slowly but steadily, the area recovered. Like so many other things that were lost in the explosion, so was the name Richmond. Today the area is simply called Halifax's North End.

FINANCIAL HELP FOR WIDOWS AND CHILDREN

At the same time the Halifax Relief Commission forged ahead with housing plans, it also began sorting through the applications and claims made for financial assistance.

In many families, the primary wage earner (usually a man in those days) had been killed. Many widows needed financial assistance for their own needs and to raise and educate their children. Survivors made applications to the commission to receive money.

The commission granted a pension to people whose husband or wife had been killed. A pension is a fixed amount of money that is paid regularly. In the case of the explosion, it was to provide relief for the loss of income resulting from the death of a husband or father. A widow received a monthly payment based on the family's income before the explosion.

The payment ranged from $40 to $65 per month; the lower amount went to people who had earned $110 or less per month. The weekly salary for a stevedore was about $20. So the payment often fell short of what the family income had been. Widows either economized or generated an additional source of income.

Getting by was a struggle for Bertie O'Brien. The monthly rent for her repaired five-room home ate up half of her monthly pension of $40. Even with her oldest girls working, to make ends meet Bertie still had to rent one of the rooms to a lodger, who paid her $3 a week. But she was a determined

People line up in relief offices to register for financial and material aid.
[City of Toronto Archives, Fonds 1244, Item 1790]

woman who succeeded and, in doing so, kept her whole family together.

If a woman remarried, she could opt for a lump-sum relief payment. For example, Elizabeth Floyd was only nineteen when her husband, Harold, was killed in the explosion. When she remarried, in 1918, she received a full settlement pension payment of $480.

Widows also received $8 per month for each child who was not old enough or physically able to support him- or herself. Orphans received $16 per month until they reached the age of seventeen, at which point they were expected to work for a living. (The pension could continue if the young adult planned to attend college and applied to the commission to do so.) If a child left Halifax, in order for pension payments to continue, the commission required that regular reports be filed to prove the child was doing well.

The Halifax Relief Commission also processed many claims for household items. The list of provisions is much the same from one family to another: clothes, furniture, and tools, everything from beds to brooms and coal for heat. The commission provided some relief to the families, but unfortunately for many, neither the monies paid nor the supplies given equaled what they had lost.

In addition to pension payments and household goods, the commission gave aid to those who had partially or totally lost their vision. Many people who stood at windows as they watched *Mont-Blanc* burn suffered eye injuries when the glass panes shattered. These injuries often resulted in the loss of an eye. About forty people were totally blinded. At the Halifax School for the Blind, adults were taught how to do tasks so they could resume household responsibilities and return to their jobs, if possible. Children learned to read and write Braille. The commission paid the housing fee for students who needed to live at the school while they studied. Edward Hartlen, the boy who had been missing for eight months before being reunited with his family, suffered considerable eye injuries. He studied at the School for the Blind for eleven months after he returned to Halifax.

Ongoing health care was a necessity for hundreds of survivors, not just those with eye injuries. Many survivors, such as Harvey MacDonald, Frances Coleman, and Phillip Hook, remained hospitalized for weeks.

The deaths and the injuries of so many loved ones devastated families, leaving the survivors overwhelmed with heartache and grief. Yet they had no choice but to continue living, taking each day as it came, hoping that with time their sorrow would become bearable.

❧12❧

TIME PASSES

LIKE A SCAB HEALING OVER A CUT, daily activities such as eating, working, going to school, and raising children wrapped themselves around sorrowful memories, quieting the pain so people could endure. Many survivors, especially those who were teenagers and older when the explosion occurred, refused to speak ever again about what had happened. They hadn't forgotten those they had lost. For them, even years later, talking about it was simply too painful. Doing so made their sadness bleed anew. Yet the only time a story or a life completely disappears is when it is no longer shared. Although many explosion stories have been lost, many still survive. Those stories live inside grandchildren and great-grandchildren, friends, teachers, and other storytellers, just waiting for an invitation to be told. Still more hide in boxes inside closets, archives, and libraries, ready for someone to find them.

Janet Kitz, a researcher and author, has lived in Halifax for many years. When she first moved there, she didn't know much about the explosion. While taking a course at a local university, a research paper about the disaster sparked her interest. And since she was married to a man who'd been born and raised in Halifax, it wasn't long before she started asking questions of survivors, some of whom were in her new family: Her husband's mother and sister had lived through it. Captivated by what she was learning, she spent hours reading old newspapers and documents. In them, she found additional stories and realized that many area residents had experiences similar to those of her relations. To preserve these stories, Kitz began interviewing more survivors. She recorded their accounts and encouraged them to share their memories with descendents and friends at gatherings, such as garden parties and reunions.

In 1918, after the unidentified dead were buried, their unclaimed effects were placed in boxes and stored in Province House, a large sandstone building where Nova Scotia's legislative assembly meets, with the hope that relatives might identify and claim them in the future. Marie Ellwood, curator of history at the Nova Scotia Museum, asked Kitz to accompany her to examine the contents of the boxes. Kitz remembers that visit, on November 27, 1981, as though it were yesterday. "We were escorted down to this rather dusty basement and saw boxes, which we opened. The first thing I picked up was a child's Richmond School notebook. On the first page was a list of spelling words that included the words: *Thou, eternity, away, forever.* Can you imagine the shudder I felt when I read that?"

The large boxes, filled with more than a hundred cloth bags and loose objects, were brought to the museum. Kitz was asked if she would be willing to catalog the possessions, assumed to be only those of the unidentified. What she discovered startled and intrigued her. "I found they were not just possessions of the unidentified. I found letters, papers, and all sorts of things with names on them." Some of the objects that included names had been placed in bags with another person's name on them. This had not been deliberately done. It happened because in some buildings a great many people died. The damage to their bodies was so severe that parts of one body were often mixed with those of others. As in the case of the notebook, at times it had been impossible to tell what effects belonged with which body. Kitz sorted and, in some cases, reassigned things according to what she discovered. In doing so, she found herself cataloging not only possessions but victims of the explosion as well.

She remembers one story in particular. A cloth bag was filled with effects that presumably belonged to a child who had lived in a group of buildings on Barrington Street. The little girl's bag contained letters addressed to Julia Carroll, a young woman who had lived in the same place. They were love letters written by Julia's husband, John, who was fighting in Europe. Julia and the couple's six-year-old daughter, Lily, were killed in the explosion. John was not allowed to return to Halifax until four months afterward. And even when he did, he never knew that Julia had saved his letters because they had been unintentionally placed in the wrong bag. The Carrolls' story, sad though it is, is only one of many that remain alive because Janet Kitz tells the tale.

As she connected items to people, Kitz occasionally discovered good news. The young Richmond schoolgirl whose notebook had contained the spelling list, for instance, had not died in the explosion. Her notebook, flung who knows how far, had simply landed near human remains, where it had been picked up and included with other unclaimed items.

The children, grandchildren, and great-grandchildren of those who lived at the time of the explosion also keep their family stories alive. While still in his teens, Harvey MacDonald—whose mother and aunt were killed in the Mi'kmaq settlement at Tufts Cove—struck out on his own, moving from Halifax to British Columbia, in western Canada, where he later married and lived a full life. Although Harvey passed away in 1991, he is remembered by his daughter. "My father always told me that even though my hair was light-colored, I reminded him of his mother Rose. He loved her so much. Sometimes he got sad because he still missed her and his brother and sister. My father named me after his mother Rose," said Rose Marie MacDonald, Harvey's oldest child and only daughter. Rose Marie gladly shares Harvey's explosion story and remembers him with love: "My father had a huge laugh that he used often, and when he hugged me, I knew I'd been hugged!" And because his grandfather Jerry Lonecloud had taught Harvey to call like a loon, Rose Marie knows how to do it, too.

According to Rose Marie, when Harvey visited Nova Scotia in 1972, he learned shocking news: His sister, Mary, and maybe even his brother, had not died in the explosion. Unfortunately, his trip to Halifax was short. He would have liked to find Mary, but he never did. Because people share stories, though, and word spreads, the families have since found each other. Rose Marie MacDonald and Carl Boutilier, one of Mary's sons, talk and e-mail regularly. From him, Rose Marie learned that Mary had indeed survived the explosion, but she had been severely burned and was hospitalized for some time. Afterward, she lived in an orphanage—a different one from where Harvey had been placed—until she was a teenager. When she left the orphanage, she married and had children. Neither MacDonald nor Boutilier has yet discovered what happened to Murray.

Lynn-Marie Richard is the assistant curator at the Maritime Museum of the Atlantic. Although the museum has a large permanent exhibit that recounts the explosion story, Lynn-Marie has an even closer connection: Gerald O'Brien—Albert and Bertie O'Brien's son—is her grandfather. "My grandfather told me that he was on the way to the store to buy barley when the explosion happened," she recalled. And he gave her something, too: the five-dollar bill that his father, Albert, had folded and tucked into his wallet the morning of the explosion. "My great-grandmother Bertie kept that five-dollar bill—a lot of money in those days—for the rest of her life. Even though she had ten children to raise and had many

This is the five-dollar bill that Albert O'Brien folded and placed in his wallet the morning of the explosion.
[Lynn-Marie and Dianne Richard]

times when she needed money." While Bertie's children were her most valued connection to Albert, the five-dollar bill was a tiny, but tangible, object that linked her with her husband on the morning he died.

Annie Pattison, Vincent's wife, and her two boys, Gordon and James, never moved back to Halifax. They remained at Annie's parents' home in Woodside. Grant Pattison, Gordon's son, has one treasured object that links him to the explosion: the watch with the distinctive cover that his father was wearing on the day of the explosion. "When I learned to tell time, my father said to me, 'Grant, this will be your watch now,'" Pattison recalled. "It was my first watch and it's precious to me."

Grant Pattison also remembers how the explosion affected his family.

> Annie, my grandmother, never got over it. She didn't talk about it at all. It was too upsetting. And every December, she became very quiet, almost a recluse. Remember, she lost a husband, a daughter, and a son. My father never talked about what

happened either. He had a nervous breakdown after the explosion. He was only fourteen years old, and he'd had to identify his father's remains all those months after the explosion. That was really hard on him. It affected him quite a bit.

Because of the trauma of that experience, Gordon left the Halifax area and lived with a relative a hundred miles away.

As Grant Pattison went on to recall, "My uncle James—Dad's brother—didn't talk much about the explosion until he met Janet Kitz. She did a wonderful thing when she interviewed him and so many other survivors and then wrote about them." After talking with Kitz, Grant's uncle James graciously shared his story of the explosion with others, particularly the tale of his book-filled leather backpack. After James had regained consciousness in the middle of the road, he was missing both his backpack and his winter jacket. During the cleanup, someone found James's bag, identifiable by his name on the books inside, and returned it to him. The outside of the pack was marred by a hole with burned edges. Whatever kind of burning debris hit the pack, it did so with enough force to cut a hole through the leather and partially through the books inside. James Pattison was convinced that if he had not been wearing his backpack, he would have been killed.

Grant Pattison fondly remembers his father, Gordon. After working on boats that traveled back and forth to the Panama Canal, Gordon settled in Dartmouth, where he became the foreman of a machine shop. "During World War II, Dad was a busy, busy man. He was in charge of getting convoy ships mechanically fit to travel at their top speed while transporting supplies for the war to Europe," Pattison said. "He and I were very close. Yep. My dad was quite a guy."

Janette Snooks willingly shares her family's story. She is the daughter of Eileen Coleman, the youngest child of Vincent Coleman, the heroic telegraph operator. Eileen had been trapped under the kitchen sink by the explosion. "Two streets in Halifax—Coleman Court and Vincent Street—have been named after my grandfather," Snooks stated with pride. "My aunt Nita, who rescued my grandmother and mother, was always willing to talk about the explosion anytime. I heard about the explosion from her. My three children often talked to her when they did projects about the explosion for school. They even recorded what she told them."

But there were lasting repercussions of that day. "My grandmother Frances [Vincent Coleman's widow] could never live in the Richmond area again," Snooks said. Several years later, Frances remarried. "James, her new husband, had been one of my grandfather's friends. His wife and some of his children had been killed by the explosion. Frances and James were married a little more than a year, when he was killed in a train accident. My grandmother never married again," explained Snooks. "In later years, she and her sister started a millinery business in Halifax. They traveled to Boston and New York to buy feathers and other trimmings for the hats they made. They became quite well known, especially by the wealthy ladies who liked . . . fancy hats."

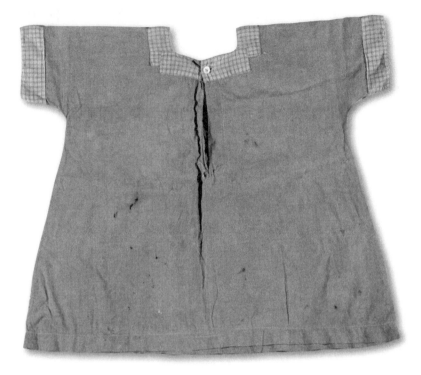

One day when Snooks was a little girl, her mother showed her a small blue dress dotted with dried blood and soot. Eileen told her daughter that it was the dress she had been wearing at the time of the explosion. After that one time, Snooks never saw the dress again, nor was it ever mentioned. "When my mother died, in 1997, I was sorting through her belongings and I found the dress. I never knew she had kept it. That's when I decided to donate it to the Maritime Museum of the Atlantic, where it would be part of their permanent display. Our family wanted everyone to see the dress, so they could know the story," Snooks said. The family also donated Vincent Coleman's wallet, which was still stuffed with papers. They hope people will remember Vincent's last moments, when he was driven by the human spirit acting at its very best.

Even in the darkest times, we look for a glimmer of hope. After the explosion, hope arrived in Halifax and Dartmouth with the outpouring of aid from strangers. Medical help, food, clothing, and supplies were part of it. In fact, the relief response to the harbor explosion serves as the model for today's relief missions. But hope came in another form as well. In reading survivor accounts, one quickly notices the frequent use of the word *kind*. Again and again, survivors mention the kindness of strangers: gentle touches, encouraging words, a shoulder to cry on, and helping hands that gave them the strength to do unbearable tasks. Amid the horror, people came together with one goal—to help those who needed it. And this part of the Halifax Harbour explosion story offers a reminder to everyone that there are times that ask us to put aside our own everyday activities and become part of a larger, human story.

Though the explosion occurred nearly one hundred years ago, people still remember: Every year, on December 6, a memorial service is held in Fort Needham Park. There, the Memorial Bell Tower stands in a direct line with the site where *Mont-Blanc* ran aground. The view is kept clear of trees and shrubbery. When the tower bells toll, the city and its people pause and remember. And every year since 1971, in Boston, Massachusetts, the city lights a freshly cut Christmas tree that towers above Boston Common. Each year's tree is a gift of thanks from Nova Scotia to the people of Massachusetts, in remembrance of the help they gave to a suffering city.

The Halifax Harbour explosion story is a tale of devastation and despair. It is equally a tale of recovery and hope. With the telling of each small story, people alive today connect with the people alive on that fateful December day. We feel their joy, their sorrow, and finally the hope that sustained them in the days that followed. Their stories become a part of us. We become a part of them. And so life continues.

Every year, on December 6, the bells in the Memorial Bell Tower ring. They can be heard all over the city. [Sally M. Walker]

The author and the shaft of Mont-Blanc's *anchor.* [James Walker]

ACKNOWLEDGMENTS

NOVA SCOTIA IS ONE OF THE LOVELIEST PLACES ON EARTH, and my family has many happy memories of the years that we lived in Halifax. Although I hadn't visited the city in ten years before I went back to research this book, as soon as I walked down the streets, I felt as though I'd come home. A number of people gave generously of their time and knowledge, none more so than Janet Kitz. She talked with me for hours about the explosion and helped me contact some of the descendants of the survivors. One crisp October morning, she walked me and my husband all around the former Richmond neighborhood, showing us where schools, homes, and churches had stood, adding more stories to my growing collection. I highly recommend the books she has written about the explosion.

Lynn-Marie Richard, at the Maritime Museum of the Atlantic, provided me with enormous help in locating photographs and showing me the unclaimed personal effects in the museum's collection. She also gave me a wonderful, unexpected surprise: her grandfather's explosion story. It was more than cool to hold the five-dollar bill and discover that Albert O'Brien and I fold paper money the same way! Thanks also to

Dianne Richard, Doug Driscoll, and Ruby Powell for providing additional snippets to the O'Brien story.

Thanks to Ruth Whitehead, Catherine Martin, and Lenny Prosper for helping me with questions about the Mi'kmaq and connecting me with Rose Marie MacDonald, who shared her father Harvey's story. As soon as she told me that her father loved to play horseshoes, I knew I'd found a kindred spirit. Rose's cousin Carl Boutilier helped round out the story with information about his mother, Mary MacDonald. Also, thanks to Roger Lewis at the Nova Scotia Museum for helping me photograph Jerry Lonecloud's moose call.

Many thanks also to Janette Snooks and Grant Pattison for sharing their families' stories. Janette is justifiably proud of her grandfather Vincent Coleman, and equally so of her aunt Nita. Both were heroes, and they made my tale richer. Grant helped me tell the story of his father, Gordon, and his uncle James and told me all about the two watches and the leather book bag. His uncle James—who looked almost exactly like my grandfather Jim—was 102 when he died in 2007.

Alan Ruffman provided great help and insight into the scientific aspects of the explosion and of the tsunami that followed. In a newspaper in musty library stacks, he rediscovered the Arthur Lismer blizzard drawing, which vividly evokes the blustery, grim day after the explosion. Thanks to Len Walther, of Northern Illinois University, for drawing the street map of the explosion area, and to Harry Chapman, who answered some Dartmouth questions.

Finding and looking through the voluminous amount of explosion material at the Public Archives of Nova Scotia would have been overwhelming, if not impossible, without the help of Garry Shutlak, George Dupuis, Barry Smith, and Gail Judge. Also at the archives, thanks to Anjali Vohra for digitally scanning photos and to Philip Hartling and Lois Yorke for research suggestions and arranging the nuts and bolts of photo permissions.

I have read nearly two hundred survivor accounts, many of which brought me to tears. It was really hard knowing the little brother or sister whom I was reading or writing about would be dead by the end of the tale. Each time I read yet another description of the impending collision of *Imo* and *Mont-Blanc*, I found myself hoping that somehow, someway, this time the ships wouldn't hit. But they always did. The explosion cloud faded away long ago. The stories of the people, however, remain strong in my heart.

SALLY M. WALKER

J. Womack

What did you want to be when you grew up?

I wanted to be a children's book author. My guidance counselor in high school said it wasn't a realistic choice for a job. Guess she was wrong.

As a young person, who did you look up to most?

One of my favorite people, whom I totally respected, was the children's librarian in my school. We had a branch of the city's public library right in my school building, so I went almost every day. Mrs. Richards knew EVERYTHING about what I liked and always had a book tucked away, waiting for me.

What was your favorite thing about school?

Hands down, my favorite subject was reading. And I snuck books into my desk to read whenever the teacher said it was time for math. Maybe that's why I later had trouble with algebra.

What were your hobbies as a kid?

As a kid I was into horses 24/7. I read about them, dreamed about them, rode them, and saved up my money until I had enough to buy one. I also loved swimming, hiking, researching local history in the library, and visiting historic places.

What are your hobbies now?

Hiking, cooking, reading, researching and visiting historic places, and Skyping with my grandson.

What was your first job, and what was your "worst" job?

My first job was walking the dog that lived next door. His name was Nikki. Shoveling manure at a horse farm may not have been the worst job I ever had, but it definitely was the smelliest.

What book is on your nightstand now?

As I type this, there are two books on my nightstand: *Ick! Yuck! Eew!: Our Gross American History*, by my friend Lois Miner Huey, and *The Lady in the Tower: The Fall of Anne Boleyn*, by Alison Weir. I love anything about the wives of Henry VIII. By the time you are reading this, I will have had at least 150 more books on my nightstand. On average, I read four or five books a week.

How did you celebrate publishing your first book?

I used the advance from my first book to buy a six-person tent, a bicycle, and a twelve-inch frying pan. I love to cook!

Where do you write your books?

The computer I work on is in my office, which was my daughter's bedroom when she was a little girl. But I often write sentences in my head when I am away from my desk.

What was your research process like for *Blizzard of Glass*?

To research this book, I read all the books about the explosion that I could get hold of. Then I went to a number of archives and libraries in the United States and in Nova Scotia and read a ton of documents. I spoke with historians and I interviewed the descendants of family members who had survived the explosion. I spoke with two survivors, but they didn't remember much since they were toddlers in 1917. I walked all over the areas of Halifax and Dartmouth that were affected by the explosion.

Can you explain what a primary source is?

A primary source is material that is written, drawn, photographed, and/or recorded by the people who personally experienced the subject. Letters, court testimony, public aid receipts, wills, photographs, and health records are examples of primary sources.

What was the most fascinating primary source you discovered?

For *Blizzard of Glass*, it was reading the accounts written by young people who survived the explosion. They described what happened to them and to their families. And it was awesome holding Gordon Pattison's watch. He was wearing it when *Mont-Blanc* exploded, and its unique cover was how his brother recognized him afterward.

What was the most difficult part of writing *Blizzard of Glass*?

It was unbelievably hard to write about Katharine and Alan Pattison. I'd gotten to know both of them through the stories their great-nephew told me. I did not want either one to die, but I had no choice.

What do you hope readers can take away from this moment in history?

I think it's very important to remember that people helping others during a time of tragedy lets survivors know that someone cares. It offers a glimmer of hope that survivors desperately need.

What advice would you give to readers who are interested in history and want to learn more about a particular topic?

Read old newspapers on microfilm and microfiche, or digitized versions of them, which might be online. Read old letters or books with transcriptions of letters. As you do this, look for the small stories—the ones you connect with on a gut level. Visit old homes, battlefields, and other places. Let the atmosphere speak to you. And ALWAYS be ready to listen to a story. That's where the passion for history starts.

What makes you laugh out loud?

Kittens at play, my two silly cats, and my grandson when he makes faces or puts underwear on his head.

What was your favorite book when you were a kid?

For years, Walter Farley's Black Stallion series and Carolyn Keene's Nancy Drew books were my favorites. My dad knew the man—yes, the man—who wrote many of the Nancy Drew mysteries.

If you could travel in time, where would you go and what would you do?

I would visit a zillion places in colonial America and get answers for the many colonial "mysteries" that I've encountered throughout my life.

What's the best advice you have ever received about writing?

The more you read, the better you will write. I'm always happy to read more; for me, books are as addictive as potato chips!

What would you do if you ever stopped writing?

I would be the best children's book illustrator in the world. Since I can't draw at all, I'd better keep writing.

SOURCE NOTES

A note about citations: In most cases, quotations have not been altered and appear as originally written or published. In a few instances, punctuation or capitalization was adjusted to accommodate the incorporation of the quotation into the text.

Unless full bibliographical information is provided in the notes below, fuller details about the sources will be found in the Selected Bibliography that follows.

Epigraph
xiii David McCullough, quoted in "The Time Machine," by Julia Keller, *Chicago Tribune Magazine*, Oct. 26, 2008, page 21.

Chapter One: A Story to Tell
1 "Since time . . .": From a letter written by Jeremiah Lonecloud in Nov. 1917. In Whitehead, *The Old Man Told Us*, page 303.

Chapter Two: Steaming Toward Disaster
13 2,925 tons: From "Explosions, Bombs, and Bumps: Scientific Aspects of the Explosion," by David Simpson. In Ruffman, *Ground Zero*, page 296.
17 "That's a . . . arrange it": Quotation courtesy of the Canadian Broadcasting Corporation from a CBC Radio Special broadcast Oct. 3, 1967, with guest Francis Mackey.

Chapter Three: December 6, 1917
19–20 Gertrude Hook Young's account: From Gertrude Young interview in Halifax Explosion Memorial Bells Committee Collection.
20–21 Descriptions of Tufts Cove Mi'kmaq settlement: From "Turtle Grove: Dartmouth's Lost Mi'kmaq Community," by Jennifer Burke. In Ruffman, *Ground Zero,* pages 45–53.

Chapter Four: In Halifax Harbour
33 "if there was . . .": Quotation courtesy of the Canadian Broadcasting Corporation from a CBC Radio Special broadcast Oct. 3, 1967, with guest Francis Mackey.

Chapter Five: Shortly Before Nine o'Clock

42 "Go on, Mack . . .": Quotation courtesy of the Canadian Broadcasting Corporation from a CBC Radio Special broadcast Oct. 3, 1967, with guest Francis Mackey.

43 Account of William Paul's actions: From *Micmac News*, "Micmacs Die in Halifax Explosion 1917," Dec. 1977, page 44.

43 Gertrude Hook Young's account: From Gertrude Young interview in Halifax Explosion Memorial Bells Committee Collection.

44 MUNITIONS SHIP ON FIRE . . . : From Kitz and Payzant, *December 1917*, page 41.

Chapter Six: A Horrendous Explosion

49 The speed of the shock wave: From "Explosions, Bombs, and Bumps: Scientific Aspects of the Explosion," by David Simpson. In Ruffman, *Ground Zero*, pages 275–299.

51 Twelve thousand buildings damaged: From MacDonald, *Curse of the Narrows*, page 66.

51 "not a piece . . .": From the report of J. Fearon, principal of School for the Deaf. Archibald MacMechan Fonds. Nova Scotia Archives and Records Management. MG 1, vol. 2124, no. 59.

51–52 Mrs. Paul's account of the explosion: From *Micmac News*, Dec. 1977, page 44.

56 "When we got . . .": From Dixon testimony, Jan. 23, 1918, for the Wreck Commission's Court. In Ruffman, *Ground Zero*, page 341.

Chapter Seven: The End of the World

59 "I thought it was . . .": From George Young interview in Halifax Explosion Memorial Bells Committee Collection.

65–66 "terrific crash . . .": From Edith Doyle interview in Halifax Explosion Memorial Bells Committee Collection.

66 Keith Allen's account: From Keith Allen interview in Halifax Explosion Memorial Bells Committee Collection.

68 Gertrude Hook Young's account: From Gertrude Young interview in Halifax Explosion Memorial Bells Committee Collection.

69 Julia De Young's account: From Julia De Young Coleman interview in Halifax Explosion Memorial Bells Committee Collection.

Chapter Eight: Help!

71 "There was no . . .": From Ethel (Kidd) Swindells interview in Halifax Explosion Memorial Bells Committee Collection.

73 "Over there . . .": From the report of Ralph Proctor. In Archibald MacMechan Fonds. Nova Scotia Archives and Records Management. MG 1, vol. 2124, no. 216.

77 Hospitals in Halifax and Dartmouth: From Kitz, *Shattered City*, page 58.

79 "Men, women . . . marveled greatly": From Willis Moore's personal narrative. In Archibald MacMechan Fonds. Nova Scotia Archives and Records Management. MG 1, vol. 2124, no. 273b.

80 Gertrude Hook Young's account: From Gertrude Young interview in Halifax Explosion Memorial Bells Committee Collection.

82–83 "I am sending...": From Metson, *The Halifax Explosion*, page 137.

83 Keith Allen's account: From Keith Allen interview in Halifax Explosion Memorial Bells Committee Collection.

Chapter Nine: A Turn for the Worse

87 "as the wagons...": From Keith Allen interview in Halifax Explosion Memorial Bells Committee Collection.

88–89 "Male, approx 38...": From identification label of Bag no. 345, Accession no. M87.2.18B. From personal communication with Lynn-Marie Richard, Maritime Museum of the Atlantic.

92 Gertrude Hook Young's account: From Gertrude Young interview in Halifax Explosion Memorial Bells Committee Collection.

93 "If You Want...": From *The Daily Echo*, Dec. 7, 1917. In Archibald MacMechan Fonds.

94 "An enormous snowdrift... the baggage car": From Ratshesky's report of the Halifax Relief Expedition. In Metson, *The Halifax Explosion*, page 139.

95 "The young man...": From Ratshesky's report of the Halifax Relief Expedition. In Metson, *The Halifax Explosion*, page 140.

96 "Women working at...": From the account of Mrs. James Slayter. In Archibald MacMechan Fonds. Nova Scotia Archives and Records Management. MG 1, vol. 2124, no. 226.

97–98 Keith Allen's account of his dog Jacky: From Keith Allen interview in Halifax Explosion Memorial Bells Committee Collection.

Chapter Ten: The Blame

99 PRACTICALLY ALL...: From *Halifax Herald*, Dec. 10, 1917, front page.

99 Description of courtroom: From "Another Calamity: The Litigation," by Donald A. Kerr. In Ruffman, *Ground Zero*, page 365.

104 Bertie O'Brien's experiences: From Lynn-Marie Richard interview with author.

104 Story of Edward Hartlen: From Mrs. Edward (Dora) Hartlen interview in Halifax Explosion Memorial Bells Committee Collection.

Chapter Eleven: Recovery and Reconstruction

107–108 Maude Fenerty's account: From Maude Fenerty interview in Halifax Explosion Memorial Bells Committee Collection.

116 Elizabeth Floyd's pension: From Halifax Relief Commission Pension Files. GSU 2312303. Files 4682–4758. Microfilm reel no. 23,168. Public Archives of Nova Scotia.

117 Story of Edward Hartlen: From Mrs. Edward (Dora) Hartlen interview in Halifax Memorial Bells Committee Collection.

Chapter Twelve: Time Passes

119–120 "We were escorted . . . names on them": From Janet Kitz interview with author.

121 "My father always . . . I'd been hugged!": From Rose Marie MacDonald phone interview with author.

122–123 "My grandfather told . . . she needed money": From Lynn-Marie Richard interview with author.

123–125 "When I learned . . . quite a guy": From Grant Pattison interview with author.

125–126 "Two streets . . . know the story": From Janette Snooks interview with author.

SELECTED BIBLIOGRAPHY

Books and Archival Records

Archibald MacMechan Fonds. Nova Scotia Archives and Records Management. MG 1, vol. 2124.

Beed, Blair. *1917 Halifax Explosion and American Response.* Halifax: Dtours Visitors and Convention Service, 2002.

Bird, Michael J. *The Town That Died: The True Story of the Greatest Manmade Explosion Before Hiroshima.* New York: G. P. Putnam's Sons, 1962.

Boyd, Michelle Hébert. *Enriched by Catastrophe: Social Work and Social Conflict After the Halifax Explosion.* Halifax: Fernwood Publishing, 2007.

Chapman, Harry. *The Halifax Harbour Explosion: Dartmouth's Day of Sorrow.* Dartmouth: Dartmouth Historical Association, 2007.

Erickson, Paul A. *Historic North End Halifax.* Halifax: Nimbus Publishing, Ltd., 2004.

Flemming, David B. *Explosion in Halifax Harbour: The Illustrated Account of a Disaster That Shook the World.* Halifax: Formac Publishing Company, Ltd., 2004.

Glasner, Joyce. *The Halifax Explosion: Surviving the Blast That Shook a Nation.* Alberta: Altitude Publishing Canada, Ltd., 2003.

Halifax Relief Commission Pension Files. MG 36, Series P, vols. 1–279. Various Files on microfilm reels. Nova Scotia Archives and Records Management.

Kitz, Janet F. *Shattered City: The Halifax Explosion and the Road to Recovery.* Halifax: Nimbus Publishing, Ltd., 1989.

———. *Survivors: Children of the Halifax Explosion.* Halifax: Nimbus Publishing, Ltd., 1992.

Kitz, Janet, and Joan Payzant. *December 1917: Re-visiting the Halifax Explosion.* Halifax: Nimbus Publishing, Ltd., 2006.

MacDonald, Laura M. *Curse of the Narrows.* New York: Walker & Company, 2005.

Mahar, James, and Rowena Mahar. *Too Many to Mourn: One Family's Tragedy in the Halifax Explosion.* Halifax: Nimbus Publishing, Ltd., 1998.

Metson, Graham, compiler and editor. *The Halifax Explosion: December 6, 1917.* Toronto: McGraw-Hill Ryerson, Ltd., 1978.

Parker, Mike. *Historic Dartmouth: Reflections of Early Life.* Halifax: Nimbus Publishing, Ltd., 1998.

Ruffman, Alan, and Colin D. Howell, editors. *Ground Zero: A Reassessment of the 1917 Explosion in Halifax Harbour.* Halifax: Nimbus Publishing, Ltd. and Gorsebrook Research Institute for Atlantic Canada Studies at Saint Mary's University, 1994.

Smith, Stanley K. *Heart Throbs of the Halifax Horror.* Halifax: Gerald E. Weir, 1918.

Whitehead, Ruth Holmes. *Tracking Doctor Lonecloud: Showman to Legend Keeper.* Nova Scotia: Goose Lane Editions and Nova Scotia Museum, 2002.

————. *The Old Man Told Us: Excerpts from Mi'kmaw History, 1500–1950.* Halifax: Nimbus Publishing, Ltd., 1991.

Newspapers and Articles

Micmac News. "Micmacs Die in Halifax Explosion 1917." Dec. 1977, page 44.

Our Dumb Animals, Feb. 1918. "The Appalling Disaster at Halifax: Massachusetts S.P.C.A. Sends Aid for Animals in Stricken City." (Public Archives of Nova Scotia: MG 1, vol. 2124 #295.)

Halifax Herald. Various issues from Dec. 6, 1917, through June 1918.

New York Times. Various issues from Dec. 7, 1917, through June 1918.

Unpublished Interviews in the Public Archives of Nova Scotia

Halifax Explosion Memorial Bells Committee Collection. Call number 1987-13 FSG 31 Sound and Moving Image Manuscript File 298-90, Mr. Keith Allen, July 24/85.

————. Call number 1987-13 FSG 31 Sound and Moving Image Manuscript File 298-103, Miss Edith Doyle, July 30/85.

————. Call number 1987-13 FSG 31 Sound and Moving Image Manuscript File 298-71, Miss Maude Fenerty, July 11/85.

————. Call number 1987-13 FSG 31 Sound and Moving Image Manuscript File 298-34, Mrs. Edward (Dora) Hartlen, July 1985.

————. Call number 1987-13 FSG 31 Sound and Moving Image Manuscript File 298-67, Ethel (Kidd) Swindells, 1985.

————. Call number 1987-13 FSG 31 Sound and Moving Image Manuscript File 298-28, George Young, July 85.

————. Call number 1987-13 FSG 31 Sound and Moving Image Manuscript File 298-29, Mrs. George (Gertrude Hook) Young, July 2/85.

Nova Scotia Archives and Records Management, Halifax Relief Commission Pension Claims. MG 36, Series P, nos. 13899, 199, and 3871.

Interviews and Personal Communications

Kitz, Janet. Interviewed Oct. 17, 2008; various e-mails 2008–2009.

MacDonald, Rose. Interviewed by phone Feb. 28, 2009; various e-mails 2009.

Pattison, Grant. Interviewed by phone Nov. 14, 2008; interviewed in person June 2009; various e-mails 2008–2009.

Richard, Dianne. Various e-mails 2008–2009.

Richard, Lynn-Marie. Interviewed Oct. 16, 2008, and June 2009; various e-mails 2008–2009.

Ruffman, Alan. Interviewed Oct. 18, 2008; various e-mails 2008–2009.

Snooks, Janette. Interviewed by phone Jan. 21, 2009; interviewed in person June 2009; various e-mails 2009.

INDEX

(Page references in *italic* refer to illustrations.)